A PSYCHIATRIST RECOLLECTS

A PSYCHIATRIST RECOLLECTS
Stories from the Lives of
Psychiatric Patients

Malcolm Baker Bowers, Jr., M.D.

New Haven, Connecticut

INSIGHT BOOKS
Human Sciences Press, Inc.

Library of Congress Cataloging in Publication Data

Bowers, Malcolm B., 1933–
    A psychiatrist recollects.

    1. Psychiatry—Case studies. 2. Psychotherapy—
Case studies. I. Title. [DNLM: 1. Mental Disorders—
case studies. WM 40 B786p]
RC465.D68   1988   616.89'09   88-2791
ISBN 0-89885-433-4

Dedicated to the memory and spirit of
Dorothea Lynde Dix 1802–1887,
mother of American psychiatry

CONTENTS

ACKNOWLEDGMENTS

I would like to acknowledge the influence and assistance of the people who have been important to the making of this book. My most fundamental debt is owed to the patients whom I have known, for it is their stories that comprise the essence of the manuscript. Norma Fox, Vice President and Editor-in-Chief at Human Sciences Press, has again been a critical voice of encouragement as well as a wise and steady guide. My gratitude also to the colleagues who have read parts of the book at various stages. Special thanks to Nancy Dunn and Peggy Weston who prepared the manuscript through a number of revisions.

Chapter 1

INTRODUCTION

The field of psychiatry is changing. Its scientific base is rapidly increasing, and the scope of its application to medicine in general is enlarging—while at the same time psychiatrists are attempting to establish a core identity and to define their relationship to other disciplines. In the midst of this ferment and debate, I believe it is critical to hold clearly in mind the kinds of human experience that lie at the heart of our task. In an era when novel enthusiasms sweep over the field with regularity, it may be useful to reflect upon the source of our commitment, which originates primarily in the lives of those we come to know well in our work, including ourselves. There is an omnipresent danger that we may drift too far from those fundamental human processes that have commanded our attention and inspired our professional lives.

This collection of accounts is, therefore, an effort to preserve some of the people and the moments I have known in my clinical work and teaching over the years. Certain elements of the life stories themselves have been changed (such as names and circumstantial and incidental details), and they are otherwise told in such a manner that the identities of the individuals upon whom they are based are protected—but their tone is faithful to the original experiences as I perceived them to be. It is primarily a book about human lives seen from the vantage point of a unique, professional perspective, while at the same time it is a statement about the learning of that perspective as I have experienced it. It is not a primer about the technicalities of psychiatric training; it is, rather, an attempt to call attention to the breadth of human phenomena that may be encountered along the way. The telling of the life stories varies from first to third person; I use the first person in some, not because they are particularly autobiographical, but because I want to highlight the experience of the psychiatrist as well as the patient. My intention is to convey the role of the psychiatrist as one who beholds, one who attends and hears, as one who therefore learns. One purpose is to convey with gratitude some of the rare privileges the profession can offer.

The training of a psychiatrist is a curious business. Most young psychiatrists-to-be do not go to medical school with psychiatry in mind. It grows on them in a variety of ways. Usually there is some mild dissatisfaction with traditional medicine, a sense that important parts of themselves are not involved in the mandated mastery of huge territories of fact and mechanism. It is a dissatisfaction that is not commonly admitted, for psychiatry is still an atypical path in the eyes of most medical educators and, consequently, in the minds of most students.

In some respects psychiatry has earned this reputation as a deviant route for a physician to pursue. Many of its practitioners seem to delight in their freedom from traditional medicine and its somewhat stereotyped roles. Helping individuals to grow psychologically, they argue, involves mobilizing latent internal forces in another human being. A therapist must keep a low profile; his efforts to guide must not compromise frail initiative. He introduces choice making as an inevitable human task, and steps back in hope that he can observe real choice occurring; for it is the act, the choosing, that makes for growth. Of course, many people engage in this guiding function and are, in one way or another, faithful to its precepts—parents, teachers, coaches, and spouses sometimes. Nevertheless the practice of professional psychotherapy requires taming and modulation of desires to control, organize, and give advice. Insofar as some psychiatrists see themselves as psychotherapists only, they pursue a professional role quite different from that of an average general physician or medical specialist. They want no part of the medical school model, which emphasizes control, advice, and prescription—never mind that this role may have been overextended, even for nonpsychiatric physicians. Being in charge is heady business; but physicians are rarely so clearly in charge. On the other hand, the passivity required at some moments in psychotherapy has too often become a posture, a kind of wordless pose that is more related to image than to therapeutic method.

Nevertheless, a psychiatrist's training is unique in all of medicine in that he must consider himself both the subject and the object of his learning. There is usually no stethoscope in his pocket and, though he should be able to perform a competent general physical and neurological examination, he typically carries around little of the characteristic hardware of the medical profession. He learns that he is his own instrument. As an observer of and participant in human experience, he must get the most out of himself—his senses, his capacity for self-reflection, and his self-control. He learns slowly and sometimes reluctantly that his responses are complex and complexly determined. In part, he perceives accurately; in part, he responds idiosyncratically, and it is precisely the untangling of the *I* from the *it* that is difficult. The other side of the matter is that he can be perceived and responded to both accurately and idiosyncratically. Thus the reality of these biases in perceiving and being perceived are slowly realized and sometimes only painfully acknowledged.

Additionally, for a psychiatrist, living and learning are uniquely bound together. There is nothing he can do to separate his own personal growth, his development as a human being, from his maturation as a professional. Here again his training contrasts with that in the rest of medicine. To be sure, many aspects of personal development color the manner in which any medical practitioner approaches his work; however, in general this influence is derivative and indirect. For a psychiatrist, the outcome of his own struggles with intimacy, disillusionment, separation, and loss directly and profoundly affect his credibility and competence. It is certain that he will not be, by wisdom or training, safe from the snares of life, much less exempt from the obligatory challenges cued by the passage of time. He will be tested as all persons are. What is crucial, however, is that he become increasingly aware in the process. Had he not chosen this field, he might expect to move through the passages of life as most people—thankfully—do. Reasonably well prepared as many are to meet personal challenges, he would likely have no cause to reflect so meticulously upon his experience or cultivate his capacity for awareness.

Such awareness develops on two levels. First, he must come to recognize by intimate encounter those forces that impinge significantly upon human lives. He must be able not only to negotiate but to recall selectively those crises and confusions of feeling that he will help others identify and name. If he cannot remember his own loneliness, he may stumble past loneliness in another life. If he cannot recall to mind the desolation of rejection, he may underestimate its power to demoralize, or overlook its hungry insistence upon speedy restitution. The other level of awareness, complementary to the first, is more precisely self-awareness. As he opens his eyes to the shrouded detail of human experience, he recognizes, always with help, that he carries unique capacities for bias and distortion. These he must learn like the contour of his body, for he cannot permit his own distortions to confuse further someone who, with his collaboration, is struggling to unravel a problem. Individuals develop these capacities slowly and with varying tempos, and maturation in these matters always extends far beyond the years of formal training. Usually the psychiatrist-in-training has only begun his task of living and learning; yet he may be asked to help those struggling with passions he has yet to encounter.

During the early years of training, a psychiatrist regularly wonders about his competence. There is a recurrent yearning for internal confirmation, some clear validation that, somewhere within, a professional identity is beginning to take shape. Here again there is a contrast with other medical specialties where the knowledge and technical proficiency required are more readily discernible. The general surgeon, for example, following his fourth or fifth cholecystectomy, can usually acknowledge a sense of emerging mastery of the procedure. Of course he realizes that there will be atypical cases, unusual patterns of bile duct anatomy, among other surprises, that he will ultimately encounter if he performs enough cases. Still, these anticipated exceptions do not seem to interfere with an early acquisition of self-confidence with respect to the overall procedure. Or the internist, after he has managed his fourth coronary or so, begins to feel the surge of assurance that comes from actually having responded intelligently and successfully to such a challenge. The psychiatrist, by contrast, can rarely count on such clear external markers of professional development. Each encounter with someone in trouble is unique enough that a foundation of generic self-confidence accrues much more slowly. Even experienced practitioners will speak of a vague sense of anxiety before they see a patient for the first time. They will speak of it, that is, if they know you well enough and trust you, for it is probably uniquely self-incriminating for a psychiatrist to admit to questions, doubts, or fears in relation to his clinical work. Lack of knowledge or technical finesse is one level of potential crticism in medicine and is painful enough, to be sure. However, the criticizing of a psychiatrist's work often involves direct or implied questions about the person himself, a step beyond the issue of knowledge or technique. So there are special vulnerabilities.

Yet there are also compensations. One of these is the progressive realization that a rare and unusual perspective upon the nature of human experience is being afforded the prepared listener, again and again, story after story. On occasion, when sitting with a person in trouble, one may suddenly sense that here—at this moment—out of the plain rendering of this or that particular circumstance or sorrow, a uniquely valid illustration of our common lot and experience has unfolded, totally un-self-consciously but with uncontestable clarity. At such times there is a longing for some way to preserve the moment, something like the photographs the plastic surgeon or the dermatologist takes, some faithful imaging, probably beyond words, and certainly beyond sound or videotape. Such moments are primarily aesthetic, as in a good dramatic scene, when the dialogue creates an authenticity that speaks directly to the most fundamental inner world of the audience. Experiences like this may play a major role in balancing the many uncertainties—professional role diffusion, loneliness,

estrangement from the core medical gestalt, to name a few—
that the psychiatrist encounters in the course of his development.
For those who cherish such surprises, there can be few com-
parable rewards.

I, therefore, offer these accounts to underscore and reaffirm
the primacy of human experience for the learning of psychiatry,
a field that is currently making genuine and significant advances.
In the context of these developments, my purpose is to restate
a fundamental perspective that we, from time to time, may be
in danger of losing.

Chapter 2

FIRST IMPRESSIONS

This initial selection of stories from the lives of psychiatric patients attempts to capture some of the human situations that a young psychiatrist likely will have to confront and to ponder from the very first day of his training. These include the struggle to find the proper distance, the wonder and terror of psychotic behavior, the ubiquity of anger and violence, the perilous meaning of family, the subtlety and power of a successful human relationship, the frustration of helplessness and failure, and the wrenching impact of suicide and death.

In the first sketch I tell of a young physician whose personal life was devastated by early symptoms of a neurological disorder. In the second, the initial impact of psychotic experience and behavior upon a young trainee is depicted. The third vignette tells of a lasting therapeutic relationship with an unmarried woman in her 70s. Linda, the fourth person described, was a young psychotic woman who first taught me about reality and fantasy in these disorders. Another patient, Viola, helped me recognize the unique importance of brief therapeutic work that may have great impact at crucial points in a individual life. Another story, of Jonathan, tells of a middle-aged man struggling for self-esteem,

17

and is concerned with problems of conflicting human values. With Frances and her sister, we detail an account of two individuals whose interdependence was played out to the end. Their devotion was for me a savage illustration of the power of human bonding. Ida Grauer tells of another form of bonding that is threatened at last by degenerative brain disease. In the story from her life, Jessie was able, despite her illness, to be a mother to her children. With Vicki, I try to relate a sense of the attrition produced by prolonged mental illness.

Captain Wilson: A Physican with Serious Illness

Captain Theodore Wilson had been diagnosed as having multiple sclerosis (MS) while he was on active duty in Europe. At first the symptoms had been subtle—some weakness in one leg, a vague sense of not being able to concentrate during dispensary hours—but when Wilson became impotent, a smoldering marital problem burst into flame. From that time on he limped slightly and was increasingly depressed. Following the spinal tap, they had told him that a diagnosis of multiple sclerosis was likely, and a protein electrophoresis of the fluid had shown a gamma-globulin elevation, consistent with that diagnosis. Wilson certainly knew the implications of his illness: most likely a protracted course, periodic exacerbations, the probability of a long period of dependent disability. Then, too, other spouses might have reacted quite differently, but Wilson's wife took his illness personally. His inactivity and complaints—most notably his impotence—became a personal deprivation to which she reacted with periodic outbursts of raging deprecation:

"Is this the best you can do? Whoever said MS affected sex? You've just given up, like you always have! Feeling sorry for yourself, that's you all right. Goddam it, Wilson, how do you think I feel? Am I supposed to go through life with you like this? . . ."

So when Wilson sat expressionless on the ward or participated half-heartedly in group discussions, others conjectured that these were the "affective manifestations of multiple sclerosis"; yet, I sensed that Wilson's hopelessness was understandable in far simpler terms. The idea of affective manifestations sounded more scientific and was also less troublesome to think about, so I accepted it along with Wilson's attempts to be collegial, even pedagogical. Our meetings, which were to discuss the administrative details of pass taking, became times for Wilson to reminisce about his medical career, and he spoke freely of the cases he remembered, his toughest diagnostic challenges, and about his secret wish to go into psychiatry. I found such apparently forthright recollections of the past comforting.

Yet when Wilson had been 4 hours late in returning from a weekend pass, I feared the outcome instinctively. Twelve hours later I forced myself to walk from the hospital to Gaetano's Funeral Home, where a hollow-eyed attendant raised a canvas sheet, and I scarcely recognized Wilson's bloated features. The moment would be forever indelible, yet always indistinct. I wanted to apologize, do penance; inwardly I knew that I had made a serious mistake in granting the pass. It turned out that Wilson's wife had driven him back from the weekend and had let him out at the front door of the hospital. A security guard had noticed that the couple appeared to be arguing. Wilson had started to enter the front door, then had turned suddenly around and headed down Harris Avenue toward the bay. He evidently rented a motel room and swallowed 12 Seconals sometime before dawn. He left no note. A very prescient senior resident was for me a great consolation. I do not know who consoled Mrs. Wilson.

ABEL: THE EXCESSES OF GUILT

Abel, a salesman, would often pace to and fro in his hospital room, lecturing, profaning, menacing, and demanding that his young doctor acknowledge the reality of his intensely felt religious experiences.

"By God, you just don't understand. You never will, you and your whole fucking crew of shrinks. You analyze everything, but I've got something you can't touch with all that Freud shit. I tell you the steeple of that church was on fire and the cross at the top was glowing red. I know what it meant—but you won't ever understand it."

I met with Abel three times a week and simply listened to this obsessed, frightened, infuriated man recount the experiences that had apparently been triggered by an act of marital infidelity. This was only confessed much later, after the acute paranoid symptoms had waned considerably following medication. The burden of guilt was real enough, one that could be understood as painful in its own right—but this, this psychic conflagration, was a completely new creation. As a match might set off a panorama of fireworks, a human event had set in motion a chain of outlandish behavior that evoked in me a profound sense of wonder, probably also of fear.

Abel went berserk on the ward one night. Apparently his delusional guilt had reached such an intensity that he had decided to kill himself. Somehow his state of mind filtered through to the nursing staff by about 9 p.m., when attendant coverage on the units was minimal. The information would probably not have upset the nurse so much had it not arrived nearly simultaneously with another report. Under usual circumstances, the charge nurse would have spoken to Abel and assessed the gravity of the situation. That night, however, she had been informed by the kitchen staff that a knife was missing from the silverware count at the same time she heard about Abel's dangerous state of mind.

By the time she had gathered together two large male attendants and the psychiatric resident on night duty, Abel had made two deep, precise, transverse incisions in both forearms. These were not scratches or superficial cuts sometimes made by some angry, demanding patients; these were acts of intense, personal loathing. As the phalanx of males cautiously approached Abel's room, they could hear him talking incoherently. His bed was the first one on the right, and as they entered the room their gaze fixed upon two rivulets of blood coursing in orderly parallel and gathering in a common pool at the foot of the bed. These streams were fed by large, pendant droplets falling from Abel's outstretched wrists, which had been almost ritualistically incised. They saw tendon, glistening white and vibrating in the dark bed of the left wrist wound. From both wrists, a steady darker ooze merged with a more pulsatile surge. Abel had indeed severed tendon, artery, and veins. Careful suturing and casting would be required and, long before he was back from surgery, the floor on the psychiatric unit had been scrubbed clean of blood.

ANNA: A FRIEND IN HER 70S

"You look very young to be a psychiatrist. Maybe I should talk with an older doctor."

"I am not as young as I look," I replied.

"Well, you're young compared to me." The lady, Anna Waters, 76 years of age, never married, complained of depression that had begun following the death of her younger sister 3 months before.

"I am an old woman—not much to live for I guess. Anyway, that's how I feel since Mary died. We were family for each other. Never had our own. Our father saw to that. He told us there were no men good enough for us. Mary had a boyfriend once, when she was 25. Father insulted him so—the one night he came to dinner—that he never came calling for Mary again. Father had become so bitter after Mother died—I was 18 and Mary was 15—that he seemed to want us to be the same."

I sat listening to this small but tastefully dressed, elderly lady recount a long simple life, sheltered by a controlling, embittered widower who had extracted every useful wifely duty from his two maiden daughters—save that of bed companion—until his death at age 90. She was my first outpatient: And as I looked at her, she seemed too small for the chair; her life too seemed to unfold as stunted, commonplace, and meticulously unfulfilled.

"After Father died, Mary and I sold the family house and bought a smaller one. We did a lot of traveling. We both loved to travel. We went to Europe five times, Japan once. I love Japan. We collected Japanese art. Had nearly four rooms full. She was all I had, Mary was."

Once a week for a month I listened to the litany of symptoms—waking every morning at 4 a.m., loss of taste for food, inability to read due to loss of concentration, complaints of failing memory. I felt more and more inadequate and helpless following each session. Anna's life had hardly ever been a life, I thought. She was right. She had lost the one meaningful person she ever had. Her depression was both understandable and inevitable.

Three weeks later, after judicious administration of antidepressant medication as suggested by my supervisor, Anna Waters wore a bright, flowery print to her session. She sounded different.

"I've been feeling better. Slept through the night last two nights. Baked a chicken last evening and invited my neighbor over. I even had a little appetite. I've been thinking a lot about Mary. Even dreamed about her. In the dream, she and I were showing report cards to Father. He seemed to be proud of Mary, carried on about how good her marks were. I kept trying to get his attention, but he woundn't pay me any mind. I think I was a little jealous of Mary right along. Do you think that's possible? She was prettier than I was. I know that for sure."

For the next three visits, Anna spoke openly about lifelong rivalry with Mary. Though always close, the sisters had competed secretly in nearly all aspects of their lives, particularly for their father's approval. I learned that often during Mary's terminal illness, when she had required Anna's constant nursing, Anna had hoped that her sister would die. She confessed these wishes haltingly, tearfully, torn by guilt.

Anna Waters got better—in fact, probably, well. She found a new live-in companion, a spinster teacher who had just moved to town, and took great pleasure in introducing her new friend to the intricacies of economy travel packages. Anna's clinical record was pulled for a formal visit only once more. However, about every 6 months I retrieved the record and added the latest postcard addressed from some Pacific island whose postage stamp was usually a large, plumed jungle creature.

Anna taught me a great deal. Because of her I never again tried to assess the value of someone else's life. I began to see that I needed to understand the structure of a life, not to judge or evaluate it—and I became fascinated by the delicate strands of meaning that could hold a life suspended above the mire of hopelessness.

Later, when I had not seen Anna for 2 years, she called for another appointment.

"I'm having some trouble, Doctor. May I see you soon?"

"Of course, Anna. What's going on?"

"I'm not sure. I just feel real down and sick. I'm not mental again, though. Very weak and tired. When can I come?"

"How about day after tomorrow at seven-thirty?"

"That'll be fine. Goodbye, Doctor."

When Anna came for her appointment, I was stunned as

she stepped into the waiting room from the parking lot. She had been driven over by her roommate, who, standing behind her, seemed to sense that Anna was seriously ill. When the light fell on her face, I noticed the unusually dark, off-color tint to her skin. Glancing quickly to her eyes, I could see that she was deeply jaundiced.

"Come on in, Anna. It's good to see you."

"I didn't think I'd ever have to come back. I was doing so good." She made her way slowly to the end room on the corridor, and seemed to wilt as she took the chair nearest the door. "About 3 months ago I started to feel weak, sorta like when I first saw you, but not exactly. Then I lost my appetite just like before and my skin began to look funny. See it now, doesn't it look dark to you?"

"Yes, it does. Have you lost weight?"

"Oh, my, yes. Nearly 10 pounds in 3 months."

Anna's diagnostic evaluation at the hospital disclosed severe anemia and liver metastases. The primary cancer was never located. When I made my first visit to Anna in the hospital, I felt frightened and helpless. At first I could not understand my reaction. Hospitals, even seriously ill patients, were no novelty. As an intern I had my share of hospital medicine and patients who were terminally ill. Now, however, I thought of myself as a psychiatrist—at least on my way to becoming one. I simply did not know what I could offer a dying 79-year-old old woman. As I entered her room, I could see that she was dozing, probably from heavy sedation. When I touched her arm, she opened her eyes and at first seemed to be bewildered, as if she did not know where she was. Then, as if the realization of her condition seeped back into awareness, she startled and appeared to recognize me.

"Hello, Doctor."

"Hello, Anna. How are you feeling?" (What a stupid question, I thought.)

"Very weak . . . and sleepy."

"Have the nurses been good to you?" (I knew I was going to run out of trite things to say very soon.)

"I'm pretty sure I'm not going to leave here."

"Why do you say that, Anna?"

"We don't have to kid each other. You and I know each

other pretty good, don't we?" Her openness put me at ease.

"Yes, I think we do."

"I want you to know that the last 2 years have been the best years of my life. Sophie and I have become the best of friends. And we've had some really great times. And you know, I've come to forgive Father. I've missed him . . . and Mary, but I haven't worried. My conscience has been peaceful. Our talks helped me a lot. I want you to know that."

I felt the tears come and took her hand and held it in both of mine, trying to decide if I should leave, afraid that I was being unprofessional.

"Anna, you have been an inspiration to me."

She closed her eyes and seemed to fall asleep. I stayed a long time holding her hand, aware that her pulse was regular, but weak and fast. For two consecutive nights I came and sat with her, but she never spoke again.

LINDA: METAPHOR AND REALITY IN PSYCHOSIS

As I entered the ward the head nurse greeted me warmly, though slightly apologetically.

"Good morning. How was your weekend?"

"Fine," I responded perfunctorily.

"Well, you have a new patient. Very interesting girl, but very sick. Came in from the emergency room on Saturday. You were up for the next admission, so you got her. You know I always look after your caseload," she teased.

"You spoil me," I teased back. "What's her problem?"

"Psychotic. Really out of it. May have something to do with drugs. Underneath she seems like a nice girl, though."

"Where is she now?"

"Room 401, sleepy. She had 300 of chlorpromazine over-night. You could probably talk to her though. Her name is Linda Scales. She's 20, I think."

I decided to go meet my new patient before rounds and the start of the day's routine—and noted that there was an uncomfortable feeling in my stomach, not unlike butterflies before a baseball game. I was beginning to realize that I usually felt anxious before meeting a new patient.

As I entered 401, I saw a young woman who appeared younger than 20 years, lying on the bed, eyes open yet fixed on the ceiling. I approached the bedside cautiously.

"Miss Scales, I'm your doctor." I walked to the edge of the bed so that I was now looking almost directly down at the young woman. If she heard me, it did not register on her face. Her eyes wandered slowly back and forth in tandem across the full range of their potential path. She was essentially expressionless except for one frightened startle she made as I tried to speak a second time. At that moment her face was instantly transformed into a mask of terror; then after several seconds she regained the appearance of imperturbability.

I thought she was catatonic so decided to be brief, knowing that her mental state was probably one of extreme sensitivity to her environment, despite her quasi-comatose state.

"Miss Scales, I think you are feeling very frightened. I'm your new doctor. You should know that you are safe here. This is a hospital and we are here to help you, no matter what your own thoughts may be telling you. I want to talk more with you whenever you feel ready."

There was no evidence that any of this little speech registered. Two months later, however, Linda Scales told me that she thought I had come that first morning to kill her with an injection. She had heard every word of my introduction and had been grateful to learn that she was not to be sacrificed, at least not right away.

After receiving medication for about a week, Linda began to speak. At first, it was only one word at a time, usually yes or no in response to a question. During the first 2 weeks I would go to her room and sit with her. If she did not want to talk I would repeat some version of that first statement to her, stay for 5 or 10 minutes and leave. After 2 weeks she was able to begin telling her story.

Linda came from a family where she was the eldest of three children. Her father was a contractor who was seldom home, her mother a vulnerable woman, chronically depressed and unhappy in her marriage, who had centered her life on her children. The family had high hopes for Linda, who had always been an excellent student. She never had many friends, however. Her dating experience in particular had been extremely limited;

somehow her mother communicated a subtle warning about men, which Linda perceived and assimilated. Three months before coming to the hospital, Linda had begun her freshman year at a college 300 miles from home. She left home feeling an inchoate sense of fear, and this fear remained with her and intensified during the first few weeks of classes.

"I couldn't sleep. When I would lie awake at night, I began to feel that something terrible was happening to my mother. I thought our house was burning. One week I called them every night to be sure they were safe. Then I began to see symbols all around that told me about my family. Bits and pieces of conversations seemed to be subtle messages from my friends, telling me about home. My roommate wore a red dress, and I thought she was telling me that someone at home was bleeding. Another friend wore white, and that meant that medical help had arrived. Finally my parents and my two brothers came to school to show me that they were all right. When I saw my mother she looked very pale, and I was certain that she had leukemia. I insisted that she go to the school dispensary and get a blood count. My fears grew worse each day, and finally my dorm director took me to the school psychologist. He told me that I would have to go to the hospital. I agreed to go, thinking it was the only way I would get medical help for my mother."

Slowly, Linda seemed to trust me. We would meet each day to evaluate her waning psychotic symptoms, and she seemed anxious to tell me about her life, particularly about her concerns for her mother. After 3 weeks we began family sessions twice a week with Mr. and Mrs. Scales. At first Mr. Scales scarcely seemed to be a member of the family. He pulled his chair back from the small circle and allowed his wife to ask and respond to questions. He would often look anxiously at Linda, but never addressed her.

"Why are you so quiet, Mr. Scales?" I inquired at the beginning of the third family meeting.

"He is always like that . . ." Mrs. Scales began.

"I'd like him to answer, if he will," I interrupted, cautiously. Linda looked increasingly anxious.

"Well, I guess Lucille is the one when it comes to the children. I just work and make the money," Mr. Scales said.

"You mean you have decided to let your wife handle all the child-rearing problems?" I persisted.

"In a way, I suppose. She was always so nervous about the children. She worries a lot."

"You never acted like you wanted to be bothered," Lucille Scales interrupted. "You just come home—usually late—eat, and look at the paper."

"I work hard, you know, honey. I'm tired when I get home."

"I'm tired too—but the kids have troubles. You just leave it all to me."

"Linda, how does this make you feel?" I interjected.

"Bad, real bad," she began to weep softly.

"Now, dear, don't cry. You are going to be all right. Isn't she, Doctor?" Mrs. Scales got up and moved toward Linda.

"I think she is also crying for you," I suggested.

"For me, what do you mean? Why for me?"

"Because you and Daddy seem so unhappy!" Linda blurted.

Over the weeks that followed, Mr. Scales was able to tell his wife in his own way that he had felt abandoned emotionally soon after Linda was born. He had decided that Lucille must have her reasons for giving the children her constant attention, so he had thrown himself into his work. Mrs. Scales was able to acknowledge that she may have become too involved in child care over the years, but that she had hoped he would be more willing to support her. She resented his withdrawal, and so became more and more child oriented. Both parents could admit their loneliness for one another. As they began to talk to one another, Linda improved perceptibly.

I was fascinated by Linda and her family. Her symptoms were clearly psychotic in the sense that they signaled a mortal danger that did not actually exist; nevertheless they embodied the essential truth of the marital impasse. In her own way, Linda had perceived correctly that it was not all right for her to leave for college. There was danger at home: not fire or serious medical illness—but rather a subtle withering of the parental bond. The strange, terrifying images of her symptoms were in reality metaphors that symbolized a much more commonplace human dilemma. So this was the meaning of her psychosis. It was as if a phantom had been unmasked and named, and that name was fear of leaving home. In a way it was the naming of the phantom that was ultimately liberating, but only after she had mourned the youthful wish that her parents' marriage be flawless. Her young mind had chosen mystery rather than grief, had embraced magic in order to ward off the pain of disillusionment.

VIOLA: FEARING DEATH AND LIFE

The first morning on the consultation service, I met Mrs. Krinsky, 47 years old, married, with a 23-year-old daughter and a 21-year-old son. One month before, she had been told that she had cervical cancer, though it was at a relatively early stage and was very likely curable with proper radiation therapy. The recommended course of treatment had been explained by the radiologist, permission slips signed, and the first treatment scheduled. However when the time came for her first radiation therapy, Viola Krinsky was unable to enter the treatment room because of overwhelming anxiety. At first the nurses had been patient, carefully reviewed what was to be done, how it would be a painless procedure, and how good the prognosis looked with treatment. But to no avail. Then the radiologist himself tried to persuade her, with considerably less patience and no more success. In his exasperation, he had threatened Mrs. Krinsky with a psychiatric consultation—by his estimation substantially more unnerving than pelvic irradiation. But Viola Krinsky was obviously mortally afraid of "hopping up on the table," as the nurses had requested, even though she knew she was in no immediate danger and that the treatments would probably eradicate her disease. The consultation request stated: "Forty-seven-year-old woman with stage 2 cervical cancer. Became hysterical when radiation started. Please evaluate."

"I feel stupid, Doctor. I never saw no psychiatrist before in my life. I don't know why Dr. Marsden sent me here, except he was pretty put out with me. But my heart was pounding so, I never was so scared, ever before," Viola Krinsky began apologetically. She had a pleasant face, round and smooth except for a few wrinkles beneath her dark eyes, wrinkles that gave her face texture and a bit of whimsy when she smiled. Her body was sturdy, compact rather than obese, and she projected a peasantlike acceptance of things as they are.

"Were you frightened of the actual treatments?" I inquired hesitantly, not knowing where to begin.

"No, I don't think so. They say radiation don't hurt, at least not while it's going on. They told me that later I might get sick to my stomach. No, Doctor, it was just fear coming on out of nowhere. 'Course the nurses thought I was afraid because I had cancer. And I was at first, when they told me, but not anymore. I know the doctors can make me well with their treatments— then I ask myself, do I want to get well? That may sound funny to you, Doctor, but I did think about that. Maybe when you have to face strong treatments, you have to want to get well real bad."

"How bad do you want to get well?" I followed her lead.

"I've thought about it some, Doctor, I'm married to an alcoholic, have been for 25 years. It's been what you could call an experience. Long time ago I told myself—I'd better not count much on Luther, that's his name—and I lived just to raise my kids. He's not a violent drunk, and he works pretty steady. Mainly he stays to himself. The kids, they're real good. Michael and Kristine. Kris graduated from high school and went to business school. Last year she married a nice fellow—works in radio and TV—they have a little place out in Pittsfield. Mike recently got his own apartment in town and has a steady job. Luther and I don't have much left between us. . . . We haven't been man and wife, you understand, in over 10 years. He never talks to me except to put me down. When I told him I had cancer of the womb, he just got angry and said, 'Once you have cancer there is nothing you can do.' "

I was drawn to the simplicity of Viola Krinsky's story. The tone did not really convey bitterness, but rather a sense of disappointment—a reluctant, yet straightforward acceptance of a limited life.

"He never gives me any support. In fact just the opposite— he keeps reminding me there's nothing to hope for. My own father died of cancer, Doctor, maybe you didn't know that. I took care of him the whole time, over 3 years it was. He had bowel cancer and they operated, left him with a bag to wear, you know. I had to watch him go from over 200 to about 100 pounds—and I had to take care of the bag, clean the place where the bag was fastened, don't you know."

While relating these details of her life, Viola Krinsky showed little emotion, and spoke almost as a nurse might describe the care of any patient with a colostomy. I decided that she was really not complaining, and wondered why.

"That must have been a terribly difficult time for you."

"Not really, Doctor. I knew my father was dying. And I knew he knew it. He needed me, though, and he used to thank me for taking care of him, used to say he knew it wasn't very pretty, the bags and all. One day he handed me a gold locket that had belonged to his grandmother—just after I had given him a sponge bath in bed. He said it was the finest thing he ever owned and he wanted me to have it." Viola's face broke for one brief moment, then she continued. "You know, Doctor, I feel like I've always just done for other folks. Some 'preciated it, like my father, and some didn't, like Luther, I guess. I don't ask for much but I do wish I had a little help when I need it . . . like now with these treatments."

"Sometimes people don't know how to help and have to be taught," I said. "Maybe Luther's like that. Maybe he needs to hear from you that you need him to help build up your hope now."

"I'm not so good at asking for favors, particularly from Luther."

"I'm not so sure that's asking for a favor. We were talking about how bad you want to get well. In the long run that depends on you, not on Luther."

A week later Viola Krinsky returned for a second visit. She reported that she had been able to complete her first radiation treatment but had been quite anxious ahead of time.

"I talked to Luther, pretty much the way you said. I don't know if it helped. He just growled and said he didn't know what the hell I was talking about. Still, he stopped talking hopeless about my treatments all the time. He even asked me where on my privates the cancer was. I drew him a picture and explained about the radiation, at least as much as I know. He's calmed down some. And I think I can get through my treatments now. . . . You know, I been thinking that I ought to pay less attention to what he says. With the kids grown up and all, maybe I should go back to work. You maybe wouldn't believe it, Doctor, but I got a job when I was 20 and saved a thousand dollars before I got married. . . ."

I did not hear from Viola again until the following Christmas. In the meantime I found out that she completed her radiation therapy without further difficulty. At Christmas, a rather ornate, religious card arrived, showing Mary, Joseph, and Jesus in a lavish manger scene complete with adoring animals. A brief note read, "Dear Doctor: I am doing pretty good, feeling stronger each day. Kris is pregnant and I have a part-time job. Thank you for listening to me. May you and your family have a nice holiday. Sincerely, Viola Krinsky."

JONATHAN: A PLACE IN THE HOUSE

He had been driven to the state hospital in an ambulance, but the scene had been a little out of the ordinary when the ambulance finally arrived at its destination. Two male attendants in whites opened the rear door, and a middle-aged man of greater than average height stepped down slowly and rather ceremoniously. He had evidently simply been sitting rather than lying down on the stretcher during the trip to the hospital, and the attendants were relaxed and informal, which meant that they were not seriously concerned about his state of mind. In the company of the attendants, he walked slowly up the steps to the admitting office. It was after dark on a Saturday night in November, and the ambulance entrance appeared well lit, almost garish in comparison with the rest of the hospital building, which was much less distinct, so that only occasional soft squares of light marked the windows of the wards. He might have been an old 50 or a young 65; it was hard to say. He was bearded and his hair was quite long, perhaps even adolescent in length and cut, suggesting a kind of unconventional, perhaps artistic lifestyle. A process of graying had begun to replace both the long hair and the beard unevenly, so that the overall effect was somewhat short of uncleanliness, perhaps closer to controlled sloppiness. He wore nondescript dark woolen pants, unsoiled but also unpressed and a bit premature for the season. Under a shapelesss and ageless brown ski parka, the edges of a faded blue workshirt were visible.

"Name?" began the night nurse, a slender black man in his 30s who covered male admissions.

No response—not so much out of defiance but perhaps more related to a wish to choose his words with great care.

"Your name, please, mister," the nurse intoned again, mechanically, but with a noticeable edge of impatience.

"Jonathan Rutherford."

"Box number?"

"We don't have one."

"You've got to have a box number, otherwise you can't get mail. Now come on, buddy, let's get on. . . ."

"We don't. We are the only place on Twin Lakes Road."

"Okay, okay, so you don't have a box number. Age?"

"Fifty-eight."

"Occupation?"

There was again a silence, longer than the night nurse would normally have tolerated, which was finally ended by a a very clear reply, spoken almost pridefully.

"Woodworker."

At that moment, one of the attendants handed the nurse an envelope containing the emergency certificate. He opened the envelope and read silently from the certificate, using a right index finger to help him locate his place while his lips moved silently, tracking the finger back and forth over the same line repeatedly.

"I don't understand this. . . . You tried to kill yourself by *not* taking your heart medicine?"

"That's correct. I have rheumatic heart disease and must take digitalis, otherwise my heart will fail."

"And why do you want to stop taking your heart medicine, mister?" The tone was challenging and more than a little sarcastic. The nurse seemed to be suggesting that the whole matter seemed a bit ludicrous, and certainly lacked the seriousness of the typical nighttime admission at a state mental hospital.

"Because my family has moved me out of the house."

The nurse raised both his hands in frustration as if to say

I give up, take this guy off my hands. "I'm sending you upstairs, Mr. Rutherford. A doctor will see you there and talk to you about your heart medicine. You'd better not bullshit him, either."

That's how I met Mr. Jonathan Rutherford. After about 2 hours together, he agreed to take his digitalis, but only after relating the following story:

Doctor, I am a real desperate man. Not so much this minute—or even today or tomorrow—but at this point in my life I will either have enough self respect to continue on or I won't.

I've struggled for most of my years and mostly I've failed. Married my wife just out of high school. She was a strong, gentle person—still is, I guess you'd say, allowing for all that's happened. Anyway, we both came from good-sized families; both our fathers were poor farmers and both were alcoholics. Never have been sure whether the stingy New England soil made 'em drink or the drink made 'em bad farmers. Hard to tell which. Anyway, both our families were poor but both our mothers held the families together somehow, enough to make us hope for something better later on. How could you even want something better out of life if somebody didn't say it could happen? That's the way I've always seen it, anyhow.

Well, we married with lots of hopes. She even talked about being a missionary. She's strong, like I said, needs a challenge. Well, I tell you the children came along and they were challenge, right enough. I'm a woodworker, carpenter you'd call it. I'm pretty good but I'm also stubborn, and about the time I'd hire on to a steady job, I'd say something smart to the boss and get fired. It was like that for most of the time the kids were young. Get work, lose it, have food for the table one week, eat oatmeal all the next. Holy shit, how did we ever survive? You know what I mean.

Then the kids would be sick. God, how I hated that. I'd be scared so I'd get angry, shout at my wife, drink too much. Once our next-to-youngest was about 10, woke up in the middle of the night all burning up. My wife, she got hysterical, called the doctor after the boy had a fit or something; he got all stiff, then shook and pissed in his pants. We wrapped him up good and drove to town. They first thought he had meningitis, but it turned out to be strep, and he was all right after he got some penicillin.

But I'll never forget what she said on our way back from the doctor's that night. "John," she said to me, "John, all my love for you is gone, just wore out. The children is all that's left to live for." Now that hurt a lot, I can tell you. But then I thought, what the hell, the kid nearly died to-night, she's had a real bad time. But you know, she moved out of the bedroom after that. A month later I bought a used bandsaw from a neighbor and set it up out in the chicken house. I decided then and there to make me a workshop.

My life got a lot more complicated after that, *our* lives did, I meant to say. But I guess I said *my* instead of *our* because that was the way it was. We both went our own way, tried to stay busy and civil to each other then, but we lived more and more at a distance. Do you know what she did then, of all things? She adopted a child. Yes, indeed. Seems that's what she did with her love, at least that's the way I saw it. The child was lovely too, a little 8-year-old Asian girl; scared to death at first, but my wife devoted herself to the girl and brought her around. Named her Tammy.

About then I started to have some luck as a woodworker, working for myself. It all started from an idea I got from a booth at the Northfield Fair one year. A guy was selling nameplates made from finished cedar strips—simple to make and he was getting five dollars for 'em. I said to myself, I could do that or something like it. Now you might say, what pride could you take in something like that, there's nothing artistic in it? But you see, that sort of thing gets you known, makes connections, people want to know what else you can do. Anyway, I started making everything from letter openers to walking sticks, and people really liked my stuff. I was finally making some money on a regular basis.

But mostly, for the first time in my life that I could remember I began to have some pride in myself. It came on slow, but I could feel it happen, and it was a real good thing for me. Just about the time my business got going, I had my first bout of heart trouble—not real serious, but a warning. The doctors told me I probably had rheumatic fever as a kid, which left me with a scarred heart valve. They said I might not need an operation if I lost some weight, watched my diet, and took my heart medicine. I took my medicine for about a year and felt so good I stopped it. In just 2 weeks I could hardly breathe, and they had to put me in the hospital. That's when my doctor told me I'd probably die if I didn't take the heart medicine. I've taken it ever since, up until 3 days ago, that is.

The rest of it is hard for me to talk about because I'm ashamed of a lot of things and I don't want to make excuses. There really aren't any excuses for some of what I did anyway. But I reckon I've been trying to fight for my life—for my life as a woodworker and a father—and it's been an uphill battle. Somehow, when my business started to do real good, I took a new look at myself in the family and didn't like what I saw. Over the years I'd become almost like one of the kids, maybe even lower down the pecking order. My wife, she tolerated me working in my shop, fed me, and was civil for the most part, but I had no say with the kids. I could have fought her, made a fuss, and I maybe should have, given the way things turned out. But I took the easy way, pretty much spent all my time in the shop. I felt good there, like I was finally somebody. No big shot, just somebody who could make things outa' wood that folks seemed to like and were willing to buy.

That was when I got my courage up to make a claim on the chair in the living room. I figured I was bringing in money on a steady basis, so I ought to be able to have a room in the house to relax. Now, from our living room you can see over 2 miles to the west down to the river, a very grand view. In winter, the corn stubble and the trees all sharp like pencils and the snow everywhere. 'Course the sunsets can be spectacular in winter, too. In spring you can follow along, week to week, the wild plums, the dogwood and lilac, and finally the laurel. Anyway, I love to sit there on an evening, smoke my pipe, and listen to classical music.

Does that surprise you?

Anyway, I told her one day as I handed her some money for groceries—timed it that way on purpose—I told her I was going to be sitting there from then on in the evenings. Sounds kinda' silly, don't it? But you get an idea how things were between us then, and how I'd become a paying boarder without much authority. She looked at me with those strong eyes, like to say, how dare you tell me what you can do in my house; then she looked down at the money in her hand, and mumbled something like, "What do I care where you sit."

At first Amy Rutherford did not return my calls, and I suspected that she was ambivalent about having her husband home, with or without his heart medicine. When I finally reached her, she admitted openly that she did not know what to do about their relationship.

"I don't know how much he's told you, doctor. . . ."

"We've only had one meeting so far."

"Then he probably hasn't told you about Tammy."

"Yes, he has—at least he mentioned her name, said you had adopted her 7 or 8 years ago."

"Is that all?"

"Well, yes, so far it is."

"Ask him to tell you the rest sometime."

"I was hoping you would come in for a talk yourself, Mrs. Rutherford."

"Not until he tells you about Tammy."

On the unit, Jonathan Rutherford was a model patient. Nursing staff quickly recognized that he was neither severely depressed nor psychotic, and they adopted a rather protective attitude toward him. In the chart they read that his problem related to his marriage and family, and, having never met his wife, they tended to regard Johathan as having been victimized in some way. They decided that he needed assertion training, and subjected him to endless group sessions in which they would attempt to challenge him to a more open expression of his feelings. Jonathan would sit, puff his pipe, and from behind clouds of smoke that smelled like fresh cedar shavings declare that it was "not seemly for a man to be emotional." Despite fervent opposition to any expression of feelings and all other similar slogans that sometimes receive a certain homage in such settings, Jonathan Rutherford was treated with substantial indulgence. That is, until he told me about Tammy.

It was quite late in the evening, and, as I recall, I was sitting at my desk in the on-call room trying to read but fighting back sleep with so little success that I had reread the same page at least three times. The phone rang and a nurse reported that Jonathan was having severe difficulty breathing. Suddenly alert, I ran down two flights of stairs to the ward and headed for his bed, where I found three female nurses trying to strap an oxygen mask over his face, which at that moment bore the expression of a man who was drowning, yet refused to cry for help.

We treated his pulmonary edema successfully, and he confessed that he had been checking his digitalis for the entire previous week. This was, of course, a well-known ruse, but somehow nobody expected it where heart medicine was concerned, despite that Jonathan had threatened exactly that before admission and had repeated his threat to the nurse who admitted him. I realized that he had lied to me, and I was furious at us both. After talking it over for nearly an hour, we both agreed it was time he told me about Tammy:

> I don't expect you to think much of me after I tell you this, Doc. There are just some things that don't ever seem forgivable when the light finally shines on them, and this, I suppose, is one of those times.
>
> My business, like I told you, got to going pretty well. I was bringing in pretty good money, enough to hold my claim on the chair in the living room, anyway. Then I worked evenings till bedtime in the shop; put in a wood stove so I could stay the long winter evenings and build my stock for the spring and summer. Even had a cot in there so I could nap if I wanted, but never gave up sleeping in the house. I'd often come up very late, but Amy never stirred a trace, though I knew she was awake sometimes. Seemed like there was more than a wall between us, more than just boards from floor to ceiling. I felt right sorry that we were so es-

tranged, I guess you'd call it, but I was holding on to my pride like a desperate man. I didn't know what I'd do if I lost it.

Anyway, that's when Tammy began to visit me in the shop. The first night she tapped on the door was one January, late, maybe 10 o'clock, snowing out. I had been working steady since after supper and had stopped a bit to build up the fire. I remember it because I first thought the knocking was the flue warming up, you know how it does. But then I realized someone was at the door. When I opened it, she stood there but didn't say a word. I recall how she looked against the white background, like a small, dark animal looking for shelter. Now she and I really had not had much to do with one another up to that time. Over the years she'd been with us, she clung pretty much to Amy, and I was content to let it be that way. After all, Amy had pretty much said that she wanted it so. Anyway, that night I invited her in, showed her some of my work, and made some tea. She was good company, never said much, but you could tell by her eyes that she was a good judge of beauty. She would take a piece I'd carved and hold it up to the light and turn it around in her hand, always smiling like she saw something there deep on the inside, something nobody else could quite make out. From then on, Tammy made a habit of coming out to my shop at night. I never asked her to, and I was surprised Amy allowed it. She was 16 and a lovely little creature; had skin the color of a light maple stain and smoother than anything you could imagine. She got to where she talked to me about all the orphanages and foster-type families she'd been put with, who had treated her fair and who had treated her bad. I guess she found me easy to talk to; I never said much when she'd get going, just nodded now and then. I used to look forward to her coming out to the shop, but we never spoke about it in the family, not to Amy for sure.

I'm not certain how we first got familiar, whether it was her or me, and it don't make a lot of difference because we both somehow accepted it as natural. We would take off our clothes and cover up by the fire with a couple of blankets in the cold weather. She seemed to want to be close to me that way, touching my skin and all. We never really had relations in the way people usually do, though we were free with each other in most every other way. It went on like that for the better part of a year, until one day Amy announced that Tammy would be going to boarding school the following week. I never learned how she found out, except I believe she knew all along. What I mean is, I wonder why she decided to send Tammy away after all. It's hard to say with a woman. Sometimes things will be settled, you know, sort of like with a set of scales, not final, but balanced off, not tipped too far one way or the other. Then all of a sudden it changes and nothing balances out any more. Then again, I thought Amy would be furious mad with me. But it was something different, more like a slow fire that just burns and burns. She could have had me arrested, you know. I guess she was too smart to call in the police, though, because that would mean I couldn't work. Amy can be a very practical woman when you come right down to it. She made her point, though. She hurt me all the more the way she did it, too, and I believe she knew it would hurt me more. She took my chair out of the living room, and she had my son Toby carry it out to the shop. She told me to sleep out there too.

You are probably wondering how I can admit to all this, and I'm sure you detest me now that you've heard it. At first, while it was happening, I had myself convinced that there was nothing really wrong with what Tammy and I were doing. Funny how you can turn things around in your own mind. There I was putting my hands all over the body of my adopted daughter, and I didn't feel any guilt—not much at first, anyway. I thought it might better be me who cared about her than some young fellow who is just using her to learn about life for himself. Then I came to believe in my mind, I really did, that for the time being at least this was the way our family had to be, maybe the best we could be just then. I thought of it as some patchwork of people and failings and wants and such as that. Seems strange now that I say it here to you. Maybe so long as I could make

myself believe that Amy saw it the same way, maybe that
was it. Anyway, when she told me Tammy would be going
away and had my chair moved, I knew the balance was gone.
More than that, I knew I had lost what I'd been working
hard for, a place to be in the house.

All I can report by way of the events thereafter is this. Jonathan took his digitalis regularly and conscientiously. I did not
feel as outraged about his revelations as I thought I should have
been, and I wondered why. I also met with Amy and Jonathan
several times together and tried to help them talk about what
had happened in a way that allowed each to give up a little but
not too much. I also negotiated successfully for Jonathan to have
his chair moved back into the living room.

FRANCES AND SISTER: STAYING TOGETHER NO MATTER WHAT

The real estate man who managed the apartments, Harry
Ives, felt that he knew Frances and her sister rather well. They
had lived in their apartment longer than anyone else in the
building—in fact, all of their lives. Before Ives had obtained the
management contract for the red-brick structure in an older
Polish section of Hartford, he had been told that the sisters were
"a little queer," but that they paid their rent on time and did
not bother their neighbors. They were the only holdover tenants,
and Ives felt somewhat protective. That was 15 years ago before,
and since then he had been into the apartment five, maybe six,
times. Before he would tap on the door at Number 2A, he would
stop to listen for conversation or any noise from inside that might
indicate that the sisters were at home. There was never any discernible sound, yet soon after knocking he could just make out
the light footstep of someone approaching to open the door.
Frances' petite gray head would appear.

"Why, good afternoon, Mr. Ives. How nice to see you. Won't
you come in?"

"Good afternoon to you, Miss Casiewski. I just dropped
around to see if everything was all right with the apartment."

"Do come in, then, and I will give you our report. Sister

and I have made a list of things that need tending, but nothing is urgent. We are managing not so bad."

The voice was soft but firm and welcoming in its own way. Ives told us that the living room, which was really as much as he ever saw of the place, always looked the same to him. He mainly remembered how dark it was. All the shades were drawn nearly to the windowsills, so that his eyes needed several minutes to accommodate to the reduced light. Frances always offered him the same chair, "Father's favorite," and apparently little used since old Casimir had died 10 years before. It was brown leather and looked in good condition except for the armrests, which were badly worn through. Frances had once explained to Ives that, "Father had a shaking palsy, and scraped the hide right off the chair here, his shaking did."

Frances struck Ives outwardly as a drab person, like the neighborhood or the old apartment building itself. Perhaps in her mid-50s, her hair remained ample though gray, and was worn pulled back in a bun, which was held in place by a white crocheted net. He could never remember her dress, and that probably says more about her appearance than any exact description could have. She was of medium height, and the only other thing Ives could remember beside the sturdy, hairy legs in dark, square-heeled pumps was her face. Frances had what he later described as a quietly zealous face. For one thing, it was full in the cheeks with large green eyes set off by full black lashes that rarely moved as she spoke. She tended to stare when she conversed, and her choice of words conveyed strong feelings under scrupulous control. But Ives could never understand what could possibly matter so much to this colorless little lady whose life seemed devoted only to the care of her sister.

There was also little to remember about the decor of the living room. Two dining room chairs with gracefully curved backs were always pulled flush to the sides of a small, cherry drop-leaf table. This table was evidently where Frances and her sister ate their meals, for there were always two place settings in view. Ives could not make out the exact color of the china; he thought it might be cobalt, but both cups and saucers as well as dinner plates and silverware were always covered by a thick embroidered napkin.

Other items that Ives recalled when he spoke with us were the family pictures of relatives in Poland, taken prior to the time that Casimir and his wife had emigrated to the States, and religious objects such as crucifixes and Bible verses, carefully lettered by hand, framed and hanging on the faded yellow wallpaper streaked here and there by water stains, which one on cursory glance might have thought were actual designs.

He also remembered Frances's sister—or Sister, as she was always referred to—for she never spoke in Ives' presence so far as he could remember. Frances would always include Sister in the conversation, but would invariably speak for her. She might say, "Sister and I went for a long walk yesterday, around by the factory and up by the church," or "Sister and I talked considerably about buying a new rug for the parlor, but then decided to wait awhile and consider our situation further." That was an expression—"consider our situation further"—that Frances would use when discussing some proposed purchase or plan.

Sister was usually lying down in one of the back bedrooms when Ives made his calls, but he remembered seeing her on two occasions. Both times she was propped up in a sitting position lengthwise on a sofa that occupied a central position against the back wall of the living room. He never saw her full in the face, for she was always presenting a side view, as arranged by Frances. Yet he remembered her profile, very different from Frances', a long, well-formed nose and a high forehead rimmed by a white skullcap, loosely-fitting, which contained under its small dome whatever hair she possessed. Ives recalled that she scarcely seemed to move, but her eyes were obviously open and appeared fixed in their gaze upon one of the myriad brown water stains on the opposite wall.

Ives learned that Sister had been a mental patient most of her life. He learned about her hospitalizations—beginning at age 18—from Frances, who spoke of her sister's illness rather openly:

"She never was a very strong child, you know. She got more colds than I did, but she was also more religious. The children teased her awfully at school. Mother used to say that Sister was like an angel who was not meant to be very much at home in the world. But we are very close—you understand that, don't you Mr. Ives? Nothing could ever separate us."

Apparently, Sister's first breakdown occurred 6 months after graduation from high school. The family had noticed that she had grown increasingly restless as graduation approached. She had made only a few friends at school, all young women her age who were nearly as shy and frightened at the prospect of adulthood as Sister was. The lucky ones got married when they finished high school. Those who were not selected at that particular point in their lives, all of them went forth into the city to find jobs, and most of them finally ended up in the screw factory.

Old Casimir had worked at Hartford Screw for over 30 years and, although the family accumulated very little over this period of time, Casimir usually spoke thankfully about his job. He would say to his wife, to Frances, and to Sister that they were fortunate to be in America, to live in an apartment, and to have food on the table. Sometimes, when he had had too much beer on Saturday night (for he only drank at home and on Saturday nights), he would curse the machines in Polish in a manner and for a length of time that which left little doubt as to his deepest feelings for his work. The girls did not understand much Polish, but they clearly understood Casimir's meaning.

Frances herself learned firsthand upon graduation of the deadly boredom of The Screw. Human robots had to stand on shift, hour by hour, and watch the ridged metalic pieces parade by on rubber conveyor belts; and it was their task to sort them according to size and to check for defects. In order to keep their sanity in the face of such relentless repetition, the sorters had learned to banter constantly back and forth, a comic improvisation that had survival value for them. They often told jokes, rather crude jokes, and delighted when the face of a female co-worker would flush crimson. The name of the factory and the major item of production made for an endless source of ribaldry, which came tumbling down the line of conveyor belts as surely as the screws themselves.

Frances had been strong enough to withstand the earthiness of The Screw, but Sister had not. Three months after beginning work there, she came home one evening and announced to Frances, while the two of them were lying in bed one night, that several male voices were in her head, repeating unspeakable obscenities over and over and over.

That is how Sister's illness began, so Frances had confided to Harry Ives after she felt that he could be trusted. Thereafter, Sister became a home-bound recluse who seemed content within the confines of the apartment and, particularly after her mother died, took on a domestic role at home and never again ventured out for the purpose of work or to widen her social world. In many respects it was quite a satisfactory arrangement; for Frances, and Casimir too until his death, worked every day while Sister watched after the apartment and prepared the meals. It was manageable—that is, except during those storms of illness when Sister would become a person transformed.

Before about 1960, when the drugs became available, she would periodically become sleepless, infuriated, outspoken, even obscene, and at these times Frances would be required to wrestle her to a back bedroom where she would stay confined behind a bolted door until the storm passed by. On these occasions, if Sister's screams became too much for the neighbors to bear during the long hours that Frances and Casimir were at work, police would be summoned to carry her away to the state psychiatric hospital, usually writhing in her own muffled screams inside a body bag. However unsettling these periods were for Frances, she never expressed to Ives the slightest resentment for Sister, even though during the psychotic relaspes she had to bathe her each day and disinfect the walls and floor of the room in which Sister had to be secluded.

After Casimir died, Frances and Sister continued to keep the apartment together. Sister's relapses seemed effectively held in check by medication that Frances administered ritualistically and with dedication. As she explained it to Ives, the two of them always played two hands of cards before retiring each night; and when the last trick had been decided, Sister would invariably ask, "Is it time for my medicine now?" This was Frances' cue to prepare the small, antique ceramic tray that had originally been fired a deep forest green laced with random golden sheaves. On the tray she would place a delicate, white lace doily brought over by their mother from the Old Country, two small tablets, and a thimble-sized crystal tumbler of brandy. During the few minutes that it took to assemble this bedside tray, her thoughts would invariably return to the other Sister, the unbridled, primitive one who used to rage and soil behind the bolted door.

Nearly 3 years before Ives' final visit, Frances retired after surviving 25 years at the factory. For the preceding 5 years she had been given a less physically demanding assignment that required only that she inspect the work of those who hovered and endured above the endless procession of screws. Following her retirement she was able to qualify for a social security payment, which, when coupled with Sister's longstanding disability check, added up to a liveable income. The two checks always appeared together on the uncovered wood floor beneath the brass mail slot for days at a time became the sisters' only conduit to the world outside their apartment. In fact it was the postman who first contacted Ives.

Ives told us that the postman called him one evening to say that he was concerned about the sisters. Ives asked him why, and was told that they must be away because the mail was rather obviously piling up on the other side of the brass slot. Ives informed the postman that it was impossible that they were away for any period of time because Sister had never been known to leave the apartment at all, and Frances would simply not allow her to be alone overnight. Ives told us that the postman also thought they might be away because of an odor that suggested there was little ventilation inside the apartment.

So Ives decided to pay an early visit to the Casiewski sisters. As he climbed the stairs to Number 2A, he felt that it was becoming unusually difficult for him to breathe. He was not one to climb stairs much, but one flight had always been something he had managed with little more than slight breathlessness. Yet as he stood on the landing in front of the sisters' apartment he found himself thoroughly winded. Even after he waited a few moments and tried to get his breath, he realized that his breathing was not improving. Then it came to him, suddenly, like waking— he did not want to breathe. At least not that air, that "awful, stinking, air," as he described it to us. His first impulse was to turn and leave, to get outside as soon as he was able in order to get away from the stench that he felt was suffocating him. Instead he reached for his handkerchief and placed it over his face and began pounding on the sisters' door, demanding that Frances open it and explain, if she could, where the odor was coming from. He said that when no one came he used his own key and unlocked the door.

Now Ives had been difficult for us to reach, you understand. All we knew at the hospital was that Frances had been brought in by ambulance; she had been picked up at her apartment after Ives called the police. Finally, several days later, we got hold of Ives, and he agreed to come to the hospital and tell us whatever he could about Frances.

He told us that upon entering the apartment he had literally been overcome by the stench. Whereas until then he had been able to breathe in small gasps through his handkerchief, inside the apartment his lungs simply refused to inspire. He remained only long enough to see Frances sitting motionless in old Casimir's leather chair while, out of the corner of his eye, he recognized a shrouded form positioned on the sofa against the back wall. All he could remember after that was wanting to run down the stairs, but being able only to inch his way down one step at a time because of his uncontrollable retching.

The coroner estimated that Sister had been dead for 8 to 10 months. But Frances insisted firmly that she had died that same day. She claimed that her sister had "got the flu, I guess. She just stayed in bed. Every day I gave her cough medicine and one aspirin. I read to her before bedtime and she coughed a lot, but finally she slept. I knew that she was getting worse, but there was nothing more I could do. After all, we only had each other and I could not leave her alone."

We did not try to talk Frances out of her rendering of Sister's illness and death. On any other subject we brought up, Frances made perfect sense. She insisted that she still wanted "to live, so I can sit, eat, and walk and remember all the good times with my sister." We found her a nursing home placement, and she seemed grateful.

At first we thought it possible to consider Frances' behavior as simply shrewd, for had she reported Sister's death, one of two checks that arrived each month would have ceased coming. But Ives put that theory to rest when he later discovered that no mail, including checks, had been opened for 6 months.

Ida Grauer: A Bond Threatened by Brain Disease

Oh, hello, Doc. This is Mr. Grauer—Ida Grauer's husband? Well, she's going to be all right; that's what the doctor at Park Ridge said, anyway. I wouldn't have called, but we had to stay in your emergency room for 6 hours last night. That's right, 6 hours. Terrible place, you know. Why, while we were sitting there waiting, they brought in a dead man from a car accident, blood all over his face. I can't tell you how upset Ida was. We were there because we didn't know where to go. A neighbor told me about your emergency room; said they had nerve doctors there who could diagnose Ida's trouble. You see, Ida's been real strange recently. She started collecting things, first little family souvenirs and things like that. But later she just kept everything— string, thumbtacks, cereal boxes, rubber bands—just junk, leastways that's what I'd call it—junk. But of course I never said that to Ida, because it would have hurt her feelings. You could tell she was serious about it and all. Must have thought it meant something special, because she fixed little piles of the stuff and talked to herself while she did—like she had an idea to make something of it, but of course she never could say what it was. Important things she forgets, though, that's how I see it. For a long time now, maybe a year, she's been asking me to do more and more little things. She always did the banking for us, took our checks down and put them on account, don't you know; but here about Christmas she just up and told me she was tired of handling all the money herself; said it was time I did my part. Now, I didn't mind so much, Doc. I like to do my share, but I had to chuckle, thinking after 40 years of being together she finally tells me to do the books. And she has been talking funny. I do notice that, to be sure. She just can't find the word she wants, or if she does it's liable to come out strange. When she finally decided to come over to your emergency room, she said it was time to go to the place where the white trucks take you that make noise if you are sick. She talks like that, uses words that aren't quite right to take the place of the ones she has forgot.

You can be sure I've been scared, Doc. How could I help it? Ida and I go back a long time. Even before we were married, our lives crossed. You probably don't believe me, but we met in Poland in a camp during the war. Lucky we didn't fall in love then. We were among the lucky few that lived through it all and finally went on to make a new life. Some who survived never came back to life. Their bodies went through the motions of living, but their spirits were dead. Anyway, Ida and I met just for a brief moment one day on kitchen detail. She was working with the cooks, and I had to bring in supplies from the truck so they could brew that awful porridge they served us. Three years later, in resettlement camp, she walked right up and introduced herself, and I could tell by that funny, crooked smile she has that it was the same girl. So wouldn't you be scared? She and I have been together so long. My mind refuses to think of life without Ida. When I try to imagine myself sitting alone at night— if she were to go before me—it all turns gray inside me and I have to throw up.

But I just wanted the doctor there in your emergency room to put her in a good hospital for a few days so we could find out why she had changed so. We were all agreed, I thought. He told me he would find a place, that it might take a little time, and that I could leave. I hated to leave Ida, but I knew she would be all right, she was in very good hands. I like that young doctor, Musselman, I believe his name is. He called and called to find Ida a place, leastways that's what he told me. And shouldn't I believe him? But no bed, no bed anywhere. Of course, I didn't know that, I'd gone home and was thinking how hard it was going to be without her, walking up and down in the house, counting the planks in our old wood floor, listening to my gypsy lullabies, records I have in Polish. They always soothe me, remind me of my mother.

You can just imagine how I felt when Dr. Musselman finally called me 4 hours later and told me they had to send Ida to the state hospital. I didn't even know where it was, and when he told me I could tell by his voice that he was uneasy. So I got scared and angry too—mainly scared—but when I get scared it comes out in anger. So that's when I called the hospital director, Mr. Anderson, and the dean, too. I was on the phone trying to reach the governor when my neighbor walked in and offered to drive me up to River Valley Hospital.

When we got there, I could not believe my eyes. I saw a sign: "Built in 1857, an Asylum for the Insane." Indeed; my Ida, in an insane asylum. So I just broke down right there and cried. My neighbor, Mr. Guzeman, had to take over for me I guess so he found the building where Ida was, sitting all by herself in a corner. She was so frightened she couldn't speak to us; she just held out both her arms as if she wanted us to take her back home right then and there.

The place was full of sad, tired people—not so many crazy ones, maybe a few—but the main feeling you had there was hopelessness, and it got into everything. The ward needed paint, the walls were dirty, the furniture broken, even the nurses— God bless them—even they seemed infected with hopelessness, as if their job was just too much for them. But, you know, they do try, they really do. I believe they have the hardest job in the world. Salvage spirits, that's what they have to do, leastways try. Well, anyway, Ida just sat there and rocked, but the chair was not a rocker; she just rocked herself, made her body go back and forth, as if she had a rhythm inside herself. The only time I ever saw that before was back in the camp, Doc, and I guess that's what finally did it for me. Ida just rocking away there, not making a sound, reminded me of that terrible time when the world went crazy, and every day I thought I would die.

I must have started yelling then—not for any particular reason, just to hear myself out loud, to be sure that I could still make a live sound. I wanted to get beyond the hopelessness and through to Ida. Well, they tied me up, after a fashion, put me into one of those shirts where you tie the sleeves? I really didn't mind it though. I mainly wanted to hear myself and wanted Ida to hear me too. All I can remember after that is somebody giving me a shot in the arm; then my eyes wanted to close real bad and they did. I guess they put me to sleep with some medicine.

When I woke up, I was home. My neighbor, Guzeman, had brought me home. He also told me that Ida was going to be transferred from River Valley to Park Ridge, a private hospital not far from our home. He said the doctors at River Valley had found out that Ida had the sugar, so that's probably the answer. That must be the reason I found all those fancy syrups and desserts around the house, hidden away in strange places. Too much sugar, that must be it, I'll bet. Guzeman told me the doctors could fix that problem in a hurry. But over there at Park Ridge they will run all the tests they need to run, from A to Z, everything. She's never been this way before, so I knew something was off. But she's going to be fine now.

Doc, I just called to tell you how Ida was coming along and to say that I was sorry if I caused you any trouble. I was pretty upset for a while, I guess. Hope the higher-ups don't give you any grief. Just tell them I said we're fine now. Ida's going to be good as new. Sure as the world.

JESSIE: A MOTHER AND A SURVIVOR

"I don't have to do nuthin' you say, Doctor. I only have to do three things—be old, be ugly, and die. . . . So don't you go round sayin' what I hafta do."

This credo was spoken under a clear-eyed stare by Jessie Sampson, in her sixth decade, in response to my going to some length to explain to her the importance of her new medication. Her face was lined like a withered apple and her cheeks were shadowy and hollow, but her intent was somehow perceived clearly by all who heard her. At first several of us were just able to suppress a laugh or at least a smile, but she seemed to gather courage as she spoke and we found ourselves being carried along. In a driven voice that almost never faltered, she remembered aloud in our presence:

> I never knew my momma. I was raised by my foster mother till I got pregnant at 18. Before that I worked in the tabaka fields and that's how I got so dark.

She had us in the palm of her very weathered hand, her natural fiery wit fed by the hot winds of the mania.

> You ain't ever worked tabaka, I bet. You couldn't do it either, probably. You hafta get up before the sun and walk out in the cool dawn. It's nice then, them big green leaves just saying good mornin' to you, Miss Jessie. You

comin' to pick us and hang us out to dry so we get all wrinkled and brown like you. What would you think, Doctor, if you was 'bout to get pulled off at the stalk, rolled up like a rug, and smoked by little bald men with potbellies hanging out over their belts?

Jessie lived with a daughter in a nearby city. She had given birth to eight children, four by her husband Calvin when they were married and four more by Calvin after he was no longer her husband.

My Calvin could work tabaka—Oh God, could he work tabaka. He'd cut twice as much leaf as any man on his plot and still be ready for me at night. Did you ever smell a man that's been cuttin' tabaka all day? Don't know why you ever would, but let me tell you he smells sweet. His body don't have no workin' smell, which I don't mind none anyway Some folks does. White folks in particular. You know what I mean, Doctor? No offense, you understand. But Calvin had that nice tabaka smell on him, real nice smell. Then I'd light him up, do you get me, Doctor? Ha, ha, I'd light him up, sure enough. . . . Those were some good times, but the babies came and I got so awful busy. We only had a two-room place at first, right there on the tabaka land. Calvin looked after the farm in the winter and I took in washing.

Jessie had apparently delivered her first four children over a 12-year span. It was after the fourth child was born, a girl named Iona, that Jessie experienced her first manic attack.

Can you ever know, Doctor, what it's like to have three little ones who need you all the time, and another one on the way? We had no money to speak of, just barely enough for food in the winter. If I wasn't a religious lady I'd of gone on beyond about then. When my time came, I had nothing left in me. They brought Iona out of me and into the world on our kitchen table. The next morning the Lord spoke to me and said, "Jessie, you got to take care of this baby," and I somehow found the strength. You won't believe the strength I had—washing, changing, cooking, chopping—

never needed to sleep. Told Calvin just what I thought too, 'bout everythin. Real snippy and uppity, he said I was. I didn't care what he thought then, anyhow. I had the spirit of the Lord in me and—I tell you the truth, Doctor—it don't matter none now whether it was true or not. It got me through for a while, gave me enough strength to feed Iona nourishment for a few months. I believe to this day I gave her just enough for her to know she had a mother. These old dried-up teats got eight little souls up and going. Pretty good, I'm thinking. But after Iona came, Calvin wouldn't let me be till I took the axe to him.

Somewhere in the fourth postpartum month following Iona's birth, Jessie, in a full manic storm, had attacked Calvin with an axe, severing three fingers on one hand. Police were summoned and Jessie was taken away to the state mental hospital. When she returned 6 months later, Calvin had placed Iona with Jessie's sister Claudia and had moved out. The three older children, a 5-year-old girl, and two boys, aged 7 and 12, remained behind in the caretaker's shack beside the tobacco field. Calvin got a divorce but continued to work the tobacco and kept the rent paid for Jessie and the children.

He told me, Calvin did, that he didn't bear me no grudge. He said he knew the Devil had me in his clutches that awful day. But he told me that he'd never be able to sleep under the same roof with me for fear I'd get the possession and come after him again. And, don't you know, Doctor, he sure was right. Every year, about March, when the snow got dirty and folks began to tap the maples up in the hills, why the sap would commence to running in me, too. And before long, the children would tell me I'd have to leave. And back to the hospital I'd go. I made about 10 visits, one a year. Then one day a new doctor, name was Fitzhugh, gave me the lithium. Told me it was almost a cure. Said it was one of nature's special secrets; promised it would calm the fire in me "like a summer shower." A bit of a poet he was, always talking fancy to me, "And now good mornin' to ya Missus Sampson. How be you on this fine day," he'd

say to me when he came round to see me on the ward. And
you know, Doctor, he was right about the lithium. That was
my last visit till this one here.

Although Calvin never moved back into the tobacco shack
with Jessie and the children, he came over often enough, and
he helped with the bills. When the oldest children were able to
work and contribute, Calvin and Jessie had four more children.
Jessie was convinced the lithium was a special gift of God destined
to help her endure the life that had come her way. So she took
it religiously, rarely missing a dose. For her it was a kind of me-
dicinal sacrament. No amount of instruction from the myriad
doctors she had outtalked and outlived could ever have provided
the conviction she possessed regarding her medication. And that
is the primary reason that she did not understand what Dr. Fitzhugh meant when, during an outpatient visit, he told her that
it would be necessary for her to take some medicine other than
lithium.

> I told Doctor Fitzhugh I need my lithium. It don't mat-
> ter none about my kidneys. It's true that a lot of water runs
> through my system. I think my kidneys must be weak be-
> cause they can't hold any water back. Dr. Fitzhugh says it's
> the lithium does that, but I don't believe it. Nothing that's
> helped me live this long gonna raise up and bite me from
> behind like that. No, sir, the lithium's my friend. Been a
> good friend for a long time. And good friends don't do you
> that way.

After 15 years without having to return to the hospital, Jessie
was found to have a severe inability to concentrate her urine, an
effect very likely due to the lithium treatment, despite Jessie's
ardent refusal to believe the connection. Dr. Fitzhugh reluctantly
decided that Jessie should stop taking lithium, given her long
period without a relapse and her excessive urinary flow. Within
5 days, Jessie was back in the hospital.

> I felt them fires coming back, too, Doctor. Just the way
> you blow on coals of a winter morning. First there is the

smoke, then the red coals aglowin', then more smoke, and
finally the fire—woosh!—it comes. And now I think my time's about over. The children are all growed mostly. And
Calvin, he's gone. Died of a heart seizure 2 years ago. I have
lived so long and now I'm ready to die. Wont do nothing
to myself but I'm tired, so very tired.

Jessie did die in the hospital 2 weeks later. Her death was
sudden and largely unexplained from a medical standpoint. All
eight children came to the hospital that night and sat together
in her room until the next morning, talking about their mother.
I met Iona then. She was a strikingly lovely girl of 19 who had
just finished high school. She told me that of all the children she
most resembled her mother.

Vicki: A Consultation

The buildings on the grounds of the Westford State Hospital
must have had a history. So many of these institutions had originally been christened with enthusiasm and hope. I recall once
seeing a foldout sketch of the Utica State Hospital in an ancient
edition of the *American Journal of Insanity*. The featured spot ac-
corded the artist's rendering and the careful, handcrafted no-
tations expressed clearly the profession's pride in the new hospital. But Westford was not 100 years old—at least these buildings
were not. Yet there had been art and theme somewhere in the
planning. The individual structures were red brick, Georgian,
several of which were fronted by white columns. If the basic ar-
chitecture retained something of a better day, everything else
about the aggregate of residential houses spoke of a minimalist
spirit, a kind of weary bureaucratic professionalism, content to
get through the day. They needed paint badly.

I drove the 30 miles to Westford on one of those late March
days that is determinedly more winter than spring. Not even the
promise of spring could alter the wintry aspect of the afternoon.
Throughout the drive I had pondered my reasons for making
the trip. The truth was that I had not wanted to go but felt obliged

to do so. I had spoken to Mrs. Iris Waldman by telephone 2 weeks earlier at the request of a colleague:

> I would be grateful to you, Doctor, if you would make a consultation for me and, I suppose, for our family. My daughter Victoria—we call her Vicki—is at Westford Hospital. She has schizophrenia. It all started when she was about 16. At least that's how it looked to everyone else, outside the family. We in the family knew that Vicki was different from almost the very beginning.

"What questions would you want me to consider, Mrs. Waldman?"

> Questions, well, let me think. . . . You see, Mr. Waldman is dead now, some 8 years, and he always hoped Vicki would recover. He said he would go to any expense. . . . She has been hospitalized 18 times. Since she was 21, she has never lived outside a hospital for longer than 3 months. And my husband was a very successful businessman. His father established a printing firm that has made money for three generations. We ran out of insurance after the fourth hospitalization. From then on everything for Vicki was out of pocket.

"What questions—"

> Oh, yes, of course, Doctor; forgive my wandering but it has been so long a time I can hardly get my mind around it, if you know what I mean. When you ask me about questions, it brings me back to reality, in a way. Makes me realize that this is just one problem, in one family. For us it has been a constant and lingering sorrow. . . . I believe it killed my husband. I think, Doctor—I think I want you to tell me if there is anything more we can do for Vicki. I am 75 years old now, and I need to know if there is anything more we can do.

I found Berkshire Hall, where Vicki Waldman had been a resident and a patient for over 4 years. I walked toward the most obvious entrance and found a hand-lettered sign taped to the door: "Entrance around the corner, in basement." And so it was, marked by an ill-fitting door that did not close completely. Once inside, I realized I was not alone. At least four individuals—patients I assumed, young, maybe early 20s—were curled up on two tattered sofas or simply lying about on a red linoleum floor, asleep or appearing to be. As I passed by, stepping over one, I heard a muffled "Hi, there," but I could not tell who had greeted me, for no one had moved. Rather awkwardly, I stopped and, trying to sound cheerful, replied to the somnolent forms, "How are all you folks?" No one stirred or answered. As I started up the stairs, however, a belated comment caught up with me.

"Asshole."

Much of the sense of desolation that pervades many state institutions arises simply because most of the buildings are empty. In the age of deinstitutionalization it has become a badge of honor for a superintendent to announce the closure of yet another building. It is not unusual to hear that a superintendent's goal is to close down an entire hospital, a kind of administrative perfection in the current manner of thinking about these institutions. Berkshire Hall was well on its way to becoming empty because whole sections of it were uninhabited. I followed the only sounds I could make out once I gained the first floor landing, and I passed through an entire ward that was completely unoccupied. No beds were present, and I was startled by the sense of space and inactivity. I walked softly, as one might walk through an old battlefield, and noted a large-lettered sign which had somehow survived on one wall: "YOU MUST TAKE YOUR MEDICATION BEFORE LEAVING THE UNIT."

On a sheet of cardboard dangling from an old piece of plywood that, I surmised, once served the functions of a bulletin board, was a crudely lettered credo:

> I believe in myself.
> There is no other way.
> Life is hard to live,
> But there are some things
> I can do to make a difference.

Brave words, I thought, but no one around to read them. As I approached the next room I could see several patients sitting drowsily in heavy chairs that were old and damaged, covered with vinyl material, wine red from age and use. One agitated man paced to and fro, gesturing menacingly with an upraised fist. No one seemed to notice him or to be concerned, as he repeated: "Goddam it to hell, you'll see, you'll see. Goddam it to hell and back!"

This room was large, too, similar to the one I had just passed through, but it was obviously inhabited. In one corner there was a nursing station marked simply by chest-high counters set at right angles that sectioned off a square of ward territory. At the junction with the wall, a hinged piece of the counter allowed access. A nurse sat busily writing and did not look up when I approached. "Good afternoon. I'm Dr. Baker, here to see Vicki Waldman. Her mother asked me to come. Did Dr. Arguella tell you to expect me?"

"No, he didn't. But it doesn't matter. We'll have to call her. Vicki is on grounds pass." She was dressed in white, no cap. A heavy, multicolored, knitted shawl was worn loosely around her neck. Forty-five, maybe, medium build. She did not look at me as she spoke. Her voice sounded perfunctory. I sensed that I was interrupting a routine.

"Goddam it to hell, you'll see, you'll see."

Uninvited, I entered the nursing station anyway and poked around a bit, hoping to find Vicki's chart. I was unsuccessful. "Could I see Miss Waldman's chart?" I asked timorously.

The nurse pushed her chair back with an air of impatience and moved slowly to a drab metal cabinet at the rear of the nursing station. She limped badly, and I noticed one obviously withered calf; probably polio, I thought. And I felt guilty for making her get up. She handed me a chart with an aluminum cover and motioned to an empty chair where I might sit.

The chart consisted primarily of state forms: Admission Checklist, Family Support Profile, Major Diagnostic Considerations Inventory, and Nursing Goals Schedule were some I came upon. Under the Doctor's Admission Form I read the following:

This is a 39-year-old unmarried chronic schizophrenic woman who has been hospitalized almost continuously since age 18. She came to Westford State from Restoration Place, a small rehab hospital in Pennsylvania. Mrs. Waldman said that the family could no longer pay the $75,000 a year that it cost there. She also said that she herself did not feel she would ever be able to care for Vicki at home. Apparently they had tried to set her up in an apartment prior to the admission to Restoration Place, but it did not work out. Vicki does not know that her mother has made this decision. . . . She is taking haloperidol 30 mg per day, which controls her more flagrant symptoms.

I became aware then that someone had approached the nursing station and was staring down at me over the wooden divider.

"Why do you read my chart?"

"Are you Vicki Waldman?"

"I am Victoria Emmons Waldman, yes. And who are you?"

"I am the doctor your mother asked to meet with you, Dr. Baker."

She was slightly stooped with almost boyish hair, short and straight. Some patients who have had to live with prolonged mental illness maintain a look of persistent youthfulness. Her face could have been that of a 20-year-old, and I noticed that her shoulders seemed rounded and that she had a prominent abdomen. Her expression was serious, even dignified, as if she were the one who was comfortable in this place and I were the outsider. Her clothes did not fit her well. She wore a pair of khaki-colored trousers that were clean but needed pressing— the kind that get washed but never ironed. Her shirt was also rumpled but clean, and unbuttoned at the neck. She had little figure to her, which suggested a mature woman. Her breasts seemed to be part of some general fullness that collected about her waist.

I have a need for Iris to support and care for me. She should no longer make me lose my freedom when it was the evil son who impregnated me with a condom in my navel.

For at least an hour, Vicki and I had a conversation about her past, mostly about her hospitalizations, although she also spoke some about her life prior to the onset of the schizophrenia. She hinted, in a rather stilted manner of speaking, that she had been afraid to leave her mother and attend school as a child.

> Iris was a warm mother, but my father was cold, and I did not want to leave her or be away from her. At school I thought only about being with my mother. The other children pushed me and called me names. When I told Iris, she would say I was not to be bothered, that she loved me, that everything would be all right.

Vicki also talked about being in psychiatric treatment from an early age, 4 or 5 years before her first hospitalization. The memory of her various therapists must have been jumbled in her mind, simply because there had been so many. She did not recall any names, but she remembered them.

> I remember my first doctor, who said I should tell him if I touched myself in my private places. There was a lady doctor who had a lisp. She reminded me of a snake.

In a variety of ways she referred several times to her father's preference for an older son. This brother was apparently the "evil son" she would mention from time to time. She periodically reverted to the litany about his impregnating her, almost as if this stereotyped allegation were an obsessional concern that required speaking at regular intervals.

Finally, she asked, "Why did you come?"

I realized that she had taken me by surprise with this most sensible of questions. I thought for several moments about the duration of Vicki's illness, the money spent, the family anguish— unquantifiable. What could I conceiveably offer in such a situation? Probably nothing, I concluded, nothing at all of a very substantive sort. But perhaps I could be the one to speak first to Vicki about a family decision that I felt had finally been made. Mrs. Waldman's question kept playing in my mind: "Is there anything more we can do?"

As I reflected upon my memory of our brief conversation, it was the tone of her voice that struck me. She was imploring me—an outsider, someone with no involvement till now and with no stake in the matter—she was imploring me to deliver a message that she felt incapable of delivering. At least that is the way I saw it.

I told Vicki then that I had come with some bad news, that her mother was older now and felt unable ever to take care of her at home. I said that when she was finally ready to leave Westford, she would probably go to a nursing home. She looked down as I spoke and did not reply right away. I had the distinct impression that she was not altogether surprised, but perhaps that was more my own wish. Finally she did speak: "This *is* bad news. It makes me enraged and sad. Why can't she take care of me?"

I replied, "I believe it is mainly because she is older and does not have the energy she used to have."

Vicki looked down and nodded as if she somehow understood and reluctantly agreed. "I knew in the days of my darkness that Mother would one day be gone. But this is bad news, very bad. I had hoped that Iris would love me and care for me all of my days," she said.

I attempted to explain that she would always have a mother who cared for her, that her mother's decision did not affect her love for Vicki. I told her that she could show her caring for her mother by continuing to make progress toward independent living. She would change the subject from time to time, either referring back to her father and the "evil son," or relating some aspect of her life in the hospital. Periodically she would return to the message I had brought, saying, "This is truly bad news." At one point, without any warning, she sat up, looked at me intently, and asked if that were all I had come to say. I nodded that it was.

> Then thank you, Doctor. You have come to tell me that Iris cannot take me home. You have brought me much sadness. I will always love my mother. If it had not been for my father and his evil son. . . . Goodbye, Doctor. Someday I may make my mother proud.

And with that, she turned and left the unit. I walked out of the hospital to my car and drove home through a late March snowstorm.

COMMENTARY

These are some of the people who have contributed to my professional development in a significant way. My contact with them varied; with some I had a closer relationship than with others. However, their stories and the lessons those stories taught have remained with me.

Captain Wilson's suicide and Abel's serious attempt in the early months of my training affected me profoundly. The suicide of a patient is probably the single most disturbing event that can occur in the professional life of a psychiatrist, and it is deeply upsetting at any point in one's career. When it occurs early, before any genuine sense of competence has accrued, it can be devastating. It did not matter that I was acting more in an administrative than a therapeutic role with Wilson, nor that Abel was in the throes of a psychotic state. These factors did not mitigate the impact of the experiences. There is indeed something unique about suicide in all of medicine from a doctor's perspective. In medicine generally, the importance of life itself is taken for granted by both doctor and patient. Together, the two are united in an effort to preserve and to enhance life. When a patient decides that he no longer wishes to live, he breaks this fundamental accord with his doctor and, in a sense, defies one of the assumptions upon which human experience is predicated. Thus the suicide of a patient not only raises questions of personal responsibility for the doctor; it also becomes an affront to the living. One's own ambivalence about the worth of human experience may be challenged. These issues can become extremely complicated and painful to unravel. I will therefore never forget the patience and wisdom of the senior resident who sat with me for several hours and helped me begin to assimilate this experience that constitutes a kind of rite of passage for the developing psychiatrist.

These stories, then, are about concerns that lie at the core of our lives, like the molten rock at the earth's core. If Wilson and Abel made it necessary for me to confront the reality of suicide, Anna and Viola surprised me from yet another dimension. I was simply incredulous that a relationship of the sort we had developed could make such a difference. I am certain that I initially began my psychiatric training with the idea that I would become a kind of psychic detective, one who first probed the emotional tangles of other people's lives and then formulated brilliant solutions. I had no genuine appreciation for the power that is latent in human contact. My experience with both Anna and Viola consisted primarily of being with them, trying to get a feeling for what really mattered to them. I sometimes did not understand what was happening between us; yet I came away convinced that something from our relationship had enabled each of them to find and explore a new dimension to their lives. This lesson often returns to mind and sustains me when I confront a clinical situation that I do not understand very well.

Linda, and Abel too, were my first encounters with true insanity, or psychosis. Their stories hopefully convey something of the truly startling nature of these conditions. Madness has always carried with it a certain seductiveness and inevitably evokes fascination as well as fear. The fascination lies, I believe, in the apprehension of a state of mind that is, on first glance, at such variance with our own. Indeed, psychotic individuals were probably the occasion for the historical origin of the term *alienist,* one who looks after those who are truly different from most other people. For students of psychopathology, perhaps even for mankind generally, explaining or rendering comprehensible such states of mind represents a distinctive challenge. Understanding madness would enable us to include within the orbit of human experience that which appears most definitively nonhuman. This desire to clarify and classify as human that which seems innately most alien can become a powerful motive for learning. Individuals like Linda and Abel represent golden opportunities in this quest.

At least two of the stories pose explicit questions about judgments of convention and morality in human relationships. Jonathan's own personal development, for all its legitimate claim, stands in sharp and disturbing contrast to his relationship with his adopted daughter. Jessie was sometimes a wild and murderous woman when she was desperately attempting to save herself and, in the best way she knew, her children. To some degree, issues of motivation and matters of behavioral standards derive from separate sources in mental life. It may be possible to understand most behavior, but all acts are not acceptable by any reasonable definition of civility. Freud's typology is sustained by a kind of face validity, for issues of need in relation to standards and to control literally become variations upon a recurrent theme as one gathers experience in the field.

Ida Grauer and Frances and Sister are stories about the bonds that human beings form. In many ways, this theme is present in every story, for it is indeed the vicissitudes of this process that make up the stories we hear from our patients every day. In these two particular accounts the focus is upon the strength and tenacity of human bonding, which is highlighted by the denial of loss or of potential loss. In psychiatry, one learns that risk and anxiety are inevitably involved in the making of a close relationship and that courage is therefore required. The more severe disorders, such as schizophrenia and related problems, lay bare the anatomy of relationship making and create renewed respect for this crucial yet complicated process. One learns, therefore, to consider respectfully the protests of people such as Frances and Ida Grauer's husband, even when they express their grief in a surprising manner.

The account of my consultation with Vicki is intended to convey something of the desolation inherent in serious mental illness, which virtually lasts a lifetime. Unfortunately, Vicki's story is not at all unusual. Many families have literally spent fortunes on the treatment of children suffering from schizophrenia or some other serious disorder. The story also attempts to portray the islands of humanity and grace that may still persist in the spirits of those who have been unremittingly ill for years.

Chapter 3

LESSONS OVER TIME

Although the initial impressions gained by immersion in the field of psychiatry may be forceful and dramatic, some of the most profound lessons can only be learned over an extended period of time. The following stories portray some of these more gradual, but no less formidable, processes encountered in the learning of psychiatry. They are concerned with such themes as the enduring character of severe mental illness, the experience of criticism and ridicule, boredom and an awareness of therapeutic limits, the bonding that time and growth can foster, the persistent intrusion of personal needs, and the emerging sense of priorities and profession.

In the first story, Elaine, I dramatize problems that are commonly encountered in therapeutic work with a group of individuals loosely termed clinically as having borderline personality disorders. In the account of Miles, I try to convey something of the tenacity and endurance required of both clinician and patient during rehabilitation from serious mental illness. With Carol, I address the difficult issue of human frailty in the lives of mental health clinicians. Randy was an older psychiatrist who made an earlier generation of practitioners and practice intensely vivid for me. The final story, concerning Ellen, tells of a young woman who had developed an acute psychotic illness postpartum and emphasizes her experience and that of others who were in close contact with her. At a more fundamental level it is a story about the irony and ambiguity that attend all levels of work in the mental health field. The final measure of one's professional maturity may be the capacity to work hopefully and persistently despite these uncertainties.

ELAINE: WHO DEMONSTRATED THE LIMITS OF THERAPY

Elaine Small was a woman in her early 20s who had been admitted following an overdose. Her father was an alcoholic, and she had become severely depressed when her boyfriend of several months had decided to call it quits. She surprised me with some typewritten pages when I introduced myself:

> I'm Elaine. This may help you understand why I'm here. I'm not so good at talking. I say things better in writing. I hope you'll read it.

> ### Drowning on Land
> by Elaine Small
>
> We come from homes
> That are whole
> And from homes that are not.
> What home is, we mirror
> For it's all we have got.

> I'm in a mental hospital. See you around, Baby. What's wrong with me? I'm not stupid or ugly! He was mine completely—short-lasting pleasure here for a moment and gone the next. So why won't you love me? I guess one body's as good as the next. That's realism. I hate myself. I am distasteful. We don't need you around here. You have no more function. I am a product of a cold rigid union the cold north wind is blowing and I feel so far away. Your body is your only asset . . . such words from a weak man. I feel like dying

or making my body ugly. Why am I so unloved when I love others and thought I was appealing? Being alone is nice sometimes not really. Open the door to hostile sounds flaring tempers flying dishes. Why do you fight? You're drunk. Mommy he's not drunk. Go to your room! Frustration tears in a torrent. But today I had good moments when a baby came running to me with arms open. It was beautiful soon as they left I was depressed more than before. I want my own baby who I can love care for and who will need love cherish me back. I love as God as People as Nature and needing and caring most of all though love me and need me. Some day I will learn to bounce back like a rubber ball instead of splattering on the floor like a smashed egg covering everyone and everything. Tears in a torrent or not at all. Sometimes I have to be scraped up like a pancake by one of the few who really cares. I would love to evaporate at this very moment . . . and at every moment of my miserable life into the thick all-enveloping air for a number of cold cruel reasons. If only I could tell maybe I will if you will only listen. I need some kind of flavoring some kind of anger some kind of truth and knowing some feeling of accomplishment and worth and really being needed by someone that I really love. My thoughts are cloudy and confused. You say you don't love me and my whole being dies little by little each day. My world is nothing without you and your love. Are you afraid of the me that I am now? Is it because I am disturbed? It is only because you have left me that I am disturbed.

I liked Elaine instinctively, and she seemed to feel comfortable with me. I was also deeply affected by the brief testimony or whatever it was that she had written. Why did this particular account get to me, I wondered? Patients often wrote about their experiences; the manics in particular. They could fill sheet after sheet of paper, and if you read the first page you had read it all. It was surely not *what* she had written, which was pretty much the sort of thing you might expect from a young girl who had been jilted.

I presented the case to a supervisor the next day. James

Freulich, M.D., who had been supervising psychiatrists-in-train-
ing for over 10 years and was highly regarded as a teacher, spoke
perfect English but with a slight European accent that conveyed
a certain formality.

"So what do you think about her, this Elaine Small?"

"She has obviously been devastated by the breakup. I'm not
sure why."

"What do you know about children of alcoholic parents? I
trust yours were not so." This guy bores right in, I thought.

"No, they weren't . . . not too much, I guess. Elaine often
talks about the conflict at home. She had to break up fights between her parents—not a pretty picture as she tells it."

"It never is pretty. These children are never allowed to be
children. They become police, arbitrators, parents to their parents. They try to bring peace where there can be no peace. They
learn to fear anger of all kinds, for they have only seen its regressive, destructive forms."

"That surely fits Elaine. In group therapy she becomes upset
when an argument erupts and tries to placate everyone."

"So why is she so lost now? This boyfriend thing, why did
it come to this? What does all this writing business tell you?"

I was not sure what Freulich was getting at. "I'm not sure
I understand your question," I began tentatively.

"In your work, Doctor, you must first become conscious of
those times when the armor of living wears thin. The average
person does not understand the perils of this life—the real perils,
that is. This is as it should be. You, Doctor, must forever put
aside this comfortable, this useful innocence. This is a vulnerable
girl, to be sure. But she is also in danger. Genuine, honest danger.
What is that danger?"

"Her boyfriend decided to leave her. Is that what you mean?"

"Ah, yes. Simple as that. But I assure you, Doctor, the frag-
mentation of love is a human catastrophe, even for a young girl
such as this. You must develop an appreciation for the pain which
the loss of love brings. Have you ever lost someone you loved
deeply?"

"No, not really. No one really close so far. I've been lucky,
I suppose."

"Indeed you have, young man. Someday, of course, you will.

Then you may understand me . . . and Elaine Small . . . and scores of others you will meet in your work. Once you appreciate her plight, you will begin to understand how her life has failed to prepare her. Without such preparation, anyone—you or I, too—can be struck down when love fails."

In the third month after discharge from the hospital, Elaine arrived on time for her appointment, dressed in a very attractive print. She was about five feet four with a round but pretty face, and her light brown hair was worn long, nearly midway down her back. A permanent frown—set, resentful and discouraged—enveloped her face like a primitive mask.

"You know, I've thought a lot about our last session. You seemed angry with me. Is that so?"

"I may have been impatient. I don't believe I was actually angry."

"Yes, you were. I know it. I can feel it when someone is angry."

"I admit you sometimes leave me feeling frustrated. Perhaps I showed it."

"Maybe I expect too much, you know. I watch everything you say, the tone of your voice, the way you look at me. . . ."

"What are you looking for?"

"I'm not sure . . . I think I want to be sure you care about me, something like that."

"Why would you wonder about that?"

"I always wonder about it . . . with everybody. I never feel secure, I'm never sure that somebody really cares. My whole life, every day is filled with trying to be sure."

"That must make you very unhappy."

"I know I'm too sensitive. But I can't seem to help it. I fall in love too easily; I know that, too. I've been seeing a fellow I met at school and I'm already too involved. But if I want to continue seeing him, I know I have to do what he wants. And *you* know what he wants."

"What do you want from him?"

"I just want him to care, to want me."

"How will you know that? How will you know if he does?"

"I guess if he says it, if he keeps asking me out."

"Do you have a feeling for the kind of person he is, the things he is interested in?"

"I really don't. We hardly ever talk. He just wants to make out."

"It sounds like you are so hungry for his affection that you can't take time to get to know him."

"I know that. But I can't help myself."

"It's really not possible for someone else to be the source of your sense of security."

"You don't think I should see him anymore, do you?"

"I think you should begin to recognize that your terrible hunger for affection has to be controlled because it gets you into difficulty."

"That's easy for you to say. But you probably have all the love you need."

"You seem uncomfortable with her," Freulich began when I presented the previous session with Elaine in supervision.

"I think I am. She seems to want a great deal from me and always leaves me feeling like I haven't helped."

"She is testing your tolerance."

"What do you mean?"

"I mean that her life experience has been one of repeated rejection. So she expects it, fears it, anticipates it, even invites it. You can best help her by not trying so hard."

"How can I not try to help?"

"That's just it. Ultimately your steadiness may help, if you can manage it. She proceeds on the assumption that you won't be able to tolerate her. No one close to her has been able to."

"So she will show me her worst to see how I react?"

"Exactly. And she will accuse you of not caring at the same time. Such patients are among the most difficult you will ever encounter."

Elaine sent me a letter in the sixth month of treatment that read in part:

> I try to block off emotions but find that I cannot change them. I often become hateful when I feel attraction. In my head at the moment is the idea that I should not be merely fond of you, but infatuated. When you first shook my hand I thought you would find it rough and would be repulsed. Can you ever understand what it's like never to be sought

after, to be homely and unbearably lonely? Everything I tell you will be so many words which you will analyze coldly. Then whatever procedures are indicated for clearing up my mind you will use. Maybe I've forced myself on you, maybe you would prefer to be rid of me. Maybe my death is the only solution. I live with a great fear—that you will laugh at me; perhaps you are laughing at me now. I am probably a ridiculous person in your eyes, good material for cruel jokes when psychiatrists get together for a drink! I can do nothing about your laughing behind my back, but someday, my fear tells me, you will laugh in my face. Once I had the impulse to sit on your lap, but this wish was suddenly swept away by the thought that I was a loathsome creature, victimizing you. It seems impossible for me to give you firm trust, friendship, unless I feel you are being given this gift by someone worthy.

I usually emerged exhausted from my sessions with Elaine but was trying to take Freulich's advice to hold fast and not react to the countless repetitive probes. She evoked in me a bewildering array of feelings—pity, guilt, affection, rage, resignation—and countless demifeelings, strange, illogical combinations of emotion that hovered just below the threshold of perception.

In the second year of treatment, Elaine died from an overdose. I did not see it coming. Freulich was painfully supportive even though I seriously considered quitting. One never forgets a suicide.

Perhaps as a form of penance, I have often attempted to go over and over in my mind our last meeting together. She had just ended a relationship that had initially seemed promising and that had in fact lasted longer than any prior involvement. The young man, Randall, was rather easy-going, a steady contrast to Elaine's erratic moods and impulsivity. For his part, he seemed to become enlivened by her emotionality, at least when she managed to keep it within reasonable bounds and did not punish him with it. However, as time went on she became dissatisfied with him, protested that he was boring and uninteresting. During some of our sessions, she seemed to recognize the pattern out of which she was responding to Randall, particularly when I pointed out the similarities to the history of our own relationship.

"Sometimes I think nothing can ever please me. In some ways I'm lucky to have Randall interested in me at all. I give him lots of grief, you know. He has stuck with me, through my tantrums and all, longer than anyone else. Except you."

"Some of this does sound familiar."

"I knew you'd say that. Maybe you have a right to. But you know . . . sometimes I think. . . ."

"You should probably finish that thought."

In my re-creation of that last session, I usually get stuck at this point. I distinctly recall that she was more open than usual, more willing to see her own actions as contributing to her deep and recurring disappointment with others. She did finish the thought, though, because I remember how troubled I was by what she said. In retrospect, not troubled enough, however.

"Sometimes I think there is nothing I can do."

"How do you mean that?"

"I have days when I see very clearly that I am my own worst enemy. I know I let my hurt become a weapon, and I drive people away . . . but, Doctor, sometimes there is just no time between."

"No time between?"

"Yeah, the hurt comes and I want to say, now watch it, you're going to be angry, you're going to react, strike out . . . and it's already too late. . . . I will have destroyed a relationship before I can catch myself. . . . What if it's always that way?"

I do not recall my answer then and I'm not surprised. I doubt that I could answer that question to her satisfaction or mine, even now.

MILES: WHO HAS REFUSED TO GIVE UP

Miles Jenkins tried to reconstruct the inexorable deterioration in his second year of college by writing down what he could remember of it:

> It all seemed to begin when I went out one Saturday night with Tom Harding. Right from the beginning I knew I was out of contact with him. I felt I could not communicate with him and it made me depressed. The whole evening he made me very uncomfortable by challenging every point I

made about the Vietnam war. I felt dominated and at a loss for words. He was degrading me, and I just wanted to get out of the restaurant. He continued, insisting that I was too timid and not really an individual. And he built himself up, told me about his success in basketball, his girlfriend, and how realistic he thought he was. I could only see him as a success and me as a failure. He just wanted to impress me. That night I walked back to school but couldn't study or read. I lost control of my emotions and began to cry a lot. When I got to my room, I found my roommate there having a discussion with two girls, and I thought they were talking about me. Every time someone would laugh, I assumed they were laughing at me, making fun of me, trying to tear me apart. I just put my head down and took what they said without a word. I remember having religious thoughts at the time. The idea came to me of kneeling in front of the cross of Jesus during a mass. I guess I realized I needed some kind of help. I remember eating some Wheaties— breakfast of champions—and I thought this was a symbolic first meal, a new beginning for me. That night I could not sleep for the second night in a row.

The next morning I decided to go home so I packed some things, and walked downtown. My mind was moving too quickly, and I felt very confused. While waiting at the bus station I began to think about my father and how I wanted to be close to him. I hoped that when I got home we could go somewhere together and talk, just the two of us. When I finally got home I felt happy, but my parents seemed surprised to see me during the middle of the week. I had the feeling I should play with my brothers and sisters, teach them, and bring harmony to the family. After the younger kids had gone to bed my father asked me if I'd been drinking. He seemed very distant, and I was disappointed that I couldn't feel close to him. I felt very uncomfortable talking to him, but he made it worse by yelling and saying that I had to open up to him and say what I thought. He apologized for never having visited me at school. I can remember only a few times when my father ever talked with me other than to give me a lecture on something or other.

The next day he said I was trying to defy him by not going back to school. I told him that I was in love with a girl at school which was a lie. I explained that I thought the sexual identities of the boys in our family were not as strong as they should be, that we were all too close to Mother. He said that perhaps he had failed, and that made me feel all the more depressed and guilty. I felt very upset, torn apart, as if the forces of love and hate were battling inside me. All the while I was home I felt much stronger and more masculine than usual. I read a sports magazine, and every story seemed to have some reference to me. I was sensitive to small noises and felt that I might be returning to my childhood. One of the stories in the magazine seemed to be ridiculing my father for the terrible way he had treated me.

When I returned to school I went immediately to the chapel where I felt safe. I felt like an infant who was making contact with people for the first time. It seemed that all the people who came into the chapel knew about me and were trying to help me. I thought my rise to notoriety began with a teacher in high school who knew all about my parents. It was as if all the people in the world were divided into two camps—those trying to help me and those trying to destroy me. Later back at my room I turned on the radio and heard a news program which seemed to be also dealing with me. The oil crisis referred to my ability to produce semen and sperm. I began to have the idea that I was in love with a girl named Jackie who was in my history class, so I went to visit her at her dormitory. Right away I told her that I loved her. She was startled and said I couldn't because I hardly knew her. I didn't fall asleep that night either.

The next day I had to register for second semester classes. Every teacher I saw registering students for courses seemed like a father figure to me. All the courses that were being offered sounded like sociology courses dealing with a case like mine. It appeared that I had changed the entire curriculum. Perhaps I had already graduated because I had taught the school something. I believed that the school was changing to create more love to improve society. The whole school must have been organized around my difficulties.

The slamming of a door meant that someone was disgusted with my actions while the constant playing of records signified that people still had hope for me. I paid close attention to the words of songs, for they seemed to be describing my life and actions.

That night again I was unable to sleep so I got up about 2 a.m. and walked downtown to a small diner. I ordered three hotdogs, thinking that they were a phallic symbol and that the number represented the Holy Trinity. When two other people walked into the diner, I became very frightened and thought they were coming in to kill me. I ran all the way back to the campus and went to the infirmary. I thought I might be dying. The male nurse took off my clothes, and I thought he wanted to perform a homosexual act. He gave me some pills, but I didn't want to take them because I thought they might be poison. I felt like a Christ figure, that I would have to die for my own good and for the good of the school. It seemed like the world was coming to an end. The next day two professors and the doctor took me to Braintree Hospital.

In the hospital they put me in a room with another patient who I felt might harm me. That night they had a family group meeting. Parents of all the patients came, and I believed they were all crazy people. Some of them seemed to act like my own parents who I thought were dead. The unit I was in contained about fourteen rooms. We had a meeting every morning to plan goals for the day. Late in the afternoon we had another meeting to review what each patient had done that day. I could not stay in the group meetings at first and often had to go to the quite room to be alone. I did not eat for the first three days. I also defecated and wet my pants several times. In the quiet room I had very strange thoughts. I believed the Bible was not a historical book but that it had just been written. I thought everyone could read my mind and would respond to my thoughts. All the noises and voices I heard were answers to my own thoughts. I believed I was being returned to my childhood.

For several days I remained in the quiet room and refused my medication, but they gave it to me by injection anyway. I began to think that the weather conditions were determined by my actions. If it rained it was because I had done something wrong. The Watergate scandal was just breaking at that time, and I thought I was responsible for it.

Finally after about three weeks I was allowed to go to the open ward. At first I was restricted to the unit, but gradually I gained more freedom. I met with a psychiatrist twice a week for about fifteen or twenty minutes. We didn't talk about anything very important, just how I was doing, how I felt about the hospital and things like that. I went swimming twice a week and took part in every activity the hospital had to offer. After about two months I was allowed to go back to school. However I found after a month or so that I couldn't do the work. I was depressed all the time, and my concentration was very poor. I slept a lot and felt very much alone. I was allowed to go home to get outpatient treatment in hopes that I could recuperate in a less demanding environment.

I first met Miles in the outpatient clinic within a week or so after he had dropped out of college. Thus began my first long-term treatment experience with a young person who had been psychotic. I had, of course, worked with several such individuals, like Linda Scales, in the hospital during the course of my training. Now, however, the task was different. The bizarre symptoms, the delusions, the crazy ideas, the chaotic amalgamation of imagination and sensation—all these had faded with medication and time—but in the aftermath of this most disruptive human experience there remained a young spirit in quiet disarray. Life had come apart just as it should have been soaring. Miles was indeed just beginning to grasp the significance of his psychotic breakdown; the task now was to help him find a path to the future. The pieces had to be put back together.

There is no simple way to convey accurately the detail of this reintegrative process, but some of my notes may provide a sense of the pattern of this particular journey.

April, 1965

He seems anxious to talk to someone; appears depressed,

perplexed. His ambivalence toward any decision is remarkable, and he constantly tries to figure out what my opinion is. Has "bonded" to me, idealized my judgment, once said "I think I'd jump off a cliff if you told me to." That makes me uncomfortable. . . . He is very hard on himself. Yesterday he called in sick at work and spent the whole session feeling guilty about it. Seemed surprised when I suggested that perhaps he deserved a day off.

Today he mentioned that the time between appointments seems very long. Talks about his exquisite sensitivity to his "relatedness" with others. Social situations, just meeting another person for the first time, these occasions are fearsome for him.

July, 1965

Good session, I thought. It focused on the idea that his relationship to me was more complex than simply good or bad. Has become involved with a young woman, Jennifer, who also has been in psychiatric treatment. They appear to cling to each other for help with the intense loneliness each feels. She can be quite cruel and critical, and he is beginning to recognize this side of her. He is slowly learning that there is real evil in the world, that all he experiences as unpleasant is not his fault. He hesitates to be open with Jennifer for fear that his lack of self-confidence will be used against him. Compares the feeling to his father's tendency to be angry with him whenever he confided weaknesses and fears. Senses that his relationship with Jennifer may be ending; he wants the relationship, yet chafes under her demanding attacks. Wonders if he can find other girls if it falls through.

March, 1966

Interesting mood variations. Now considerably less depressed, even a little high, cocky. Talks of being able to blow up at his boss (partially justified, it seems to me). Says he feels "separate" (he used this word several times) from others, in a good sense. Appears to mean that he is bothered less by the tyrannical self-scrutiny that has plagued his relationships. Has apparently successfully terminated the relationship with Jennifer and begun a new friendship with a girl named Celia. At the beginning of each relationship his fantasies tend to run away with him. His intense neediness seems to burst its barriers and literally has him going steady, having sex, and contemplating marriage in the course of a few days! I think back to my own crushes—were they really so different? I don't know, although at least I recognize some of his feelings. He sent me a letter recently describing his "growth spurt," as he put it:

> I want to describe for you how my feelings and thoughts about myself and my world have changed recently. The first person this change affected directly was Jennifer. I now feel separated from her. I have deep feelings for her, but I also have a strong need to be free to be with other people. I feel differently about women generally, don't see them now simply as sex objects but also as people that I can get to know. I also find that I can stand up for myself more easily. I'm not afraid to be honest with people, to tell them where my head is. I feel more like an individual. I feel like I have more a mind of my own, and I hope that it will show. I no longer feel that you are perfect or are some sort of wizard. This feeling makes me more comfortable with you. I also think I am better at evaluating people, less naive, you might say. Generally I like people a lot, but I don't trust blindly the way I used to. I may get carried away with my angry feelings sometimes. I feel a strong need in my head to be able to stand up to you, to be on equal terms with you. This may be some kind of turning point where I am no longer intimidated by you. I feel less need for your constant approval; you are less of a father figure to me now. But I regard you very much like a friend.
>
> One thing that bothers me is the fantasies I have been having recently. The idea comes to me often that I will become famous because of my beliefs and philosophies, that I will defend innocent people—women, homosexuals, shy and inhibited people. In recent weeks I have had more energy than before and seem to require less sleep.

June, 1966

The mood swings are very obvious to me now. When he is

depressed he feels an acute lack of confidence, has little social interest, wants to sleep a great deal. At the other extreme he is cocky, self-assured, socially active, if not overactive, and tends to be unable to sleep. It is impressive that his mood can so markedly affect his feelings about himself and can determine his social style.

January, 1967

Has met a new girl, Gloria. She seems quite reasonable, honest, and open. He is not rushing in so headlong this time. Recently spent an interesting week at home and suddenly seemed to notice the importance of his mother in his life. Feels she has "attached herself to her children as if they were her whole life." Sees her as totally gratifying the children's needs, leaving his father to be "the bastard." Feels her influence may have made him crave the approval of women, and yet be very vulnerable to rejection. His overall state of increased arousal continues. He is overly self-conscious, intensely aware of the feelings of others, senses that he is "almost paranoid." I have trouble knowing whether his insights are valid or not. They seem to occur mainly when he is somewhat high, yet they also appear to be accurate for the most part. Can they do him any good? I don't know the answer yet.

May, 1967

Continues to see his mother as "totally accepting," not fostering independence. She created in him a sense that he was "special." Also notes that he never regarded her as a "sexual person." A recent date with Gloria was upsetting. She came on very aggressive sexually, and he was taken aback, didn't want to think of her as someone who "fucked guys." Somehow he got his mother involved in his thoughts here, the idea that a woman should not be "just for sex." Sent me another letter dealing with this recent period:

> I need to sort out on paper some feelings that I have
> been having. They are complex and sometimes quite con-

fusing. Much of my rapid growth recently has had to do with an intense sexual awareness. The beginning of all these feelings took place during a recent visit home when I began to see that my mother had enmeshed herself in her children's worlds. Furthermore I believe that my close ties with my mother have robbed me of a normal and healthy sense of my own sexuality. She has always appeared asexual to me and in actuality is filled with guilt about the whole matter of sex. I believe my father is much the same. Currently my sexual appetite is very strong, and I find myself thinking that I am a sexual animal. I think constantly about mating, fucking, survival, self-preservation. I am more conscious of setting boundaries, distance, and territory between me and others, men especially. I feel good—at times lonely—but more capable of reaching out to others. I have also been more acutely aware of the way my father behaves. He is the great intervener—"Don't do that, be careful, watch out," etc. He is very uptight and rarely in a good mood.

I always seem to be searching for a mothering woman and feel easily rejected when a woman doesn't accept me quickly. However, there is a kind of paradox here. If a woman wants me too quickly, I get equally anxious. I have a very difficult time establishing a deeper-than-friendship relationship with a woman. At times I feel painfully vulnerable, that I almost have no control. I think this may be partly normal in establishing a relationship—the give and take of gut communication. However I feel the whole process is very slow for me. My moods frighten me too. Sometimes I feel the strength to make my own decisions, other times I am crippled by self-doubt.

June, 1967

Talks of an improved relationship with his employer whom he sees somewhat more realistically. His boss seems genuinely interested in his development at work. Talked of a recent experience with Gloria. They got involved in some petting but decided to "cool off." He talks in terms of wanting to "be in control," which seems to mean not letting himself get too needy or too vulnerable. Just beginning to realize that he can (and must) exert control over the pace of relationships. Reported a dream in which I was hurt and taken to a hospital. He felt numb and abandoned, was upset at the intensity of his reaction to my injury in the dream. Afterward talked of the "dangers of being too close."

August, 1967

Actually did quite well during my vacation (2 weeks), but he broke up with Gloria over this period. He said he "hurt a lot" but was not incapacitated. Reported another dream in which he was sitting in my lap and I asked him if he wanted to be a baby. He talked about the dream, then mentioned the possibility that he could see me less frequently. (I guess my vacation had more effect than either of us realized.) He wondered whether I was influencing him too much.

January, 1968

Realizes that he has tended to "dump" his moods in my lap, expecting me to do something. Mentions more sense of responsibility for his state of mind. He talks of wanting to be more in charge of himself and not depend on me. Has begun group therapy in addition to his sessions with me. Finds initial relief that others have similar concerns, that they will support him when he is feeling bad.

March, 1968

With difficulty I brought up the issues of his unpaid treatment bill. (Even with a fee reduction, he has accumulated an unpaid balance of over $300. The family is no help here at all. They have made it clear that he will have to pay for treatment himself.) He was surprised; I sense that he has never considered that I might make requests of him. Nearly 3 years now we have been meeting. Sometimes I wonder if I have been any help at all. He *has* remained out of the hospital and has worked most of the time. I think there has been some progress in his understanding of other people and consequently in his gratification from them, and I believe the group work has been a help. Much more work to be done in this area, no doubt. He sent me another progress report:

> Since the beginning of group therapy (about three months ago) I have noticed an increased sense of stability in my life. In the beginning I was afraid to open up, but I soon became comfortable being a member of a small group. I have discovered that understanding from the group is more important (and possible) than complete acceptance. I think that is an insight I will have to remember for the rest of my life. I am also doing better in expressing my anger in the group, particularly when I am up front about my feelings but under control. My moods don't control me as much as they used to. I don't feel so hopeless when I am depressed but realize that I must do something then. I am a little more assertive with women but I still have problems in this area. I seem to need something from them so desperately, yet real closeness with a woman scares me.

I worked with Miles for over 8 years. And for many more thereafter, when he was very much on his own in the world, he would send me cryptic notes at unpredictable intervals, as if I were an old and trusted friend.

CAROL: WHO FORGAVE GRACIOUSLY

First Session

"I'm not sure if I should be here or not. I mean, I know I have to do something. . . . I can't continue as I am; I feel tired all day, don't have any appetite. I guess I'm depressed. Anyway my GP said it was all psychological. He did lots of tests and everything was all right. Thyroid, blood count, you know. So I talked it over with my husband, and we decided to call the clinic for an appointment."

"When did you begin to feel sick . . . or depressed?"

"I believe it has been coming on gradually, now that I think back. Maybe 6 months, maybe a year. I think it kinda slipped up on me. It has been pretty hard in the past 2 years. I have two young kids—a girl 7 and a boy 4—who keep me pretty busy. I have a good husband. . . . I don't have any reason to be depressed, at least none I know of. I just feel run down, worn out . . . and pretty guilty about being this way."

"Can you tell me a little about yourself? Where you grew up, for example."

"Well, that's a long story and not one I like to think about. I feel like that's all behind me. At least I hope so. But if you think it would help. . . . I was born in a small town in central Massachusetts, Smithville. My father owned a garage but he drank a lot. There were three of us kids; I was the oldest. My mother just tried to keep body and soul together. There would be long periods when my father wouldn't be working. There was never much business, but when something turned up, he was usually too drunk to do the work. My mother took in laundry, and I helped her. We just about made meals and rent. Finally my father just disappeared—I was 11 then. We haven't heard from him since. There was a rumor that he was in Boston for a while living with a woman. I never saw him again though, and he never tried to come back. . . . Anyway, Mother took a job as a waitress, and I kept the laundry business going myself. You might say we were poor—dammed poor. Somehow we survived, though. I went to the high school in town, made good grades, and planned to go to college. Tom, my husband, was my high school sweetheart, and I got pregnant my senior year. We decided to get married because we eventually planned to anyway. I miscarried after 3 months that first time, though. We've been married now for 8 years. It's been good, not so easy, but I think we have a pretty good marriage, considering. Tom's not very ambitious but he's good to me and the children."

Carol Smythe related this background information during her first session. She was a strikingly attractive brunette with a serious, tired expression. Although dressed in modest clothes, her tall, slender figure gave her a certain elegant bearing. She spoke softly, almost in a whisper. Her psychiatrist found himself responding with sympathy and a strong wish to help.

Second Session

"Talking with you last time was a great relief. I realize I've never had much of an opportunity to talk about myself. I really enjoyed it. Is that wrong?"

"Why would it be wrong?"

"Oh, I don't know. Maybe it's selfish. I mean I've always had to think about taking care of other people—first mother and my brothers, now Tom and the kids. It just seems like an indulgence to talk about myself."

"Maybe it's long overdue, that you give yourself some time."

"It seems like a luxury. I thought going to a psychiatrist would be painful, scary, you know. That's what you hear, anyway."

"I'm glad you haven't found it that way."

"Well, I do feel guilty. Spending money on myself, just for talking. I think I never had anyone listen to me the way you do. Most of my life people have been asking things of me—chores, meals, that kind of thing. Even my mother, when I was young she was always so tired I never felt right telling her about my problems. Not that I had any real big ones. . . . I guess I was disappointed about not going to college. Maybe that was a problem. I wanted to be a physical therapist. I knew I'd have to forget about that, though, after I missed my period in my senior year. It was the first time Tom and I had made love. We were both so scared. I wasn't even sure he had come inside me. I prayed he hadn't, every night I prayed. When my period didn't arrive I waited 2 weeks and told Mother. I'll never forget what she said. 'Well, dear, I guess we don't have to be worrying about money for college now.' That was all she said."

"You must have felt pretty bad."

"Then when I told Tom, I knew he was awful upset. He didn't speak to me for about a week. Then one Sunday he drove over and announced that we would get married. It was a rush job after that. You know how it is in a small town."

Third Session

"I had a dream last week. It was really weird. I was in a

strange town filled with people milling about. Only everyone was a man. All the faces appeared the same and none of them would look at me. Then all of a sudden I saw my father walking toward me. At first I thought he recognized me but then he just walked on by as if he hadn't seen me. I started crying and woke up. I had actually been crying in my sleep."

"What stands out in your mind about the dream?"

"Stands out? Well I guess the strongest feeling was the excitement I felt seeing my father. Then the disappointment that he didn't recognize me . . . or didn't seem to. . . . Once when I was 10 we had planned a family picnic. Mom and I had worked all morning, making sandwiches and baking cookies. I was so happy because she said Daddy would be going with us. We waited and waited for him to come home from the garage, but he never did. Mom went downtown and came home crying. She said Daddy would not be coming with us. She had found him drunk at a bar around the corner from the garage. I can remember the disappointment to this day. . . ." She began to weep softly, unable to continue.

After several minutes, her psychiatrist said, "You still feel the disappointment very deeply."

"I'm sorry . . . I can't seem to get hold of myself."

"You needn't apologize."

A Session Near the End of Four Months of Treatment

She had been a very enthusiastic and gratifying patient. The therapy had consisted primarily of her developing an awareness of a wish for a strong, benevolent, paternal figure in her life, and the relationship of this wish to her experience with her father seemed clear enough. Marriage to a childhood sweetheart had really not provided a solution, for her husband was somewhat passive and looked to Carol for guidance and structure in the marriage. Her psychiatrist was aware of the positive feelings she had for him as a transference object, but was only dimly conscious of his vulnerability to her idealized view of him. His response was to push for a speedy termination.

"You seem very thoughtful tonight," he began cautiously.

"I have been thinking a lot about our sessions, wondering if I have made progress."

"It seems to me that you have," he replied. "You've certainly worked hard. How do you see it?"

"You have helped me a great deal. Talking with you has been an unusual, a wonderful experience."

"You sound like you might be ready to try it on your own," he said, conscious that he was nudging.

"Do I? Do you think I'm ready, I mean cured?"

"Cure is a tricky notion in this kind of thing. I do think you have a new grasp of your problems."

"You almost sound like you are trying to get rid of me," Carol said teasingly but with a detectable note of disappointment.

"Only if you feel strong enough to try it on your own. . . . Of course, if things don't go well you can always come back, and we can pick up where we left off," he replied in a slightly defensive tone, aware that she had detected his pressure for termination, a pressure he recognized but did not fully comprehend.

"Then perhaps I should try it," she said. "You know I will never forget you. You have made me realize what it can be like to be totally open, to be free with my feelings. . . . I don't know how to thank you."

"I will miss our talks, too," he confessed, wishing as he spoke that he could withdraw these words that sounded too personal, maybe even entreating.

Carol did not let him take them back, but rather seized upon their latent meaning. "Do you really mean that?" she said. "Could I really mean anything to you?"

Throughout this interchange he had felt himself slipping. The sensation was strange, frightening, yet thrilling. His thoughts seemed to surge ahead of him, careening dangerously, like a car out of control. On occasion, thankfully only a few, his attention lapsed and he felt his own need rise within, grasping for space, demanding for himself that which he was attempting to provide for others. By an effort of will he silently shouted himself down. It usually worked, or had until this moment. There was something about Carol Smythe—the way she openly confessed her affection, the way she looked at him without reservation. Although he was relatively inexperienced, he sensed the threat to his professional role. It was unthinkable that he would ever misuse or misappropriate a therapeutic relationship.

"Well, of course, I mean . . . all my patients mean a great

deal to me . . . he retreated, covering his route with a platitude.

"I see . . . I thought . . . of course . . . that is, I hoped you might consider me special," Carol blurted out with disarming honesty.

"You are special, each person is special because each person is unique," he fought to regain some degree of professional distance. He was beginning to feel safe. Like someone who had been gravely tempted to steal but who instead had turned at the last moment and fled the scene of his temptation, his anxiety lessened with each unit of time and space he was able to interpose.

Carol, too, sensing his struggle and feeling a surge of pity as well as shame, regained her own composure. "Perhaps you are right. Maybe it's time for me to go it alone. I hope I won't have to . . . I mean . . . I guess I want to say I know I have to leave treatment sometimes. . . . Anyway, thank you."

"I hope it goes well. Let me know if I can help further."

Two months after apparently terminating treatment, Carol Smythe called for an appointment. He had vaguely expected her to return at some point, but he was not prepared for what happened. When he walked to the waiting room to meet her, she was not seated but rather was standing uneasily, smoking a cigarette. He could not help notice her figure, slender but full in the hips, accentuated by a pair of very tight white slacks. Her blouse was satiny, a flowered print, disarmingly loose and open at the collar.

"Won't you come in, Carol." He welcomed her in a forced, overly professional tone.

She entered the consultation room, but remained standing, looking directly at him.

"Please sit down," he offered, surprised that he needed to make the suggestion. She did not follow his invitation.

"I don't want to take up too much of your time. I haven't really come to resume therapy. In fact, I've been doing quite well . . . except. . . ."

"Except?" he queried nervously.

"Except . . . I can't put you out of my mind," Carol blurted out. "I really can't. I think of you all the time. During the day, with the children, out driving—you're like an obsession. I can't help it, so I decided I would come and tell you about it."

He felt suddenly extremely lightheaded. His legs seemed

frail enough to give way at any moment. He was the first to sit.

Carol continued. "I know I'm putting you on the spot. I'm sure most of your patients don't do this. . . . I mean don't come into your office and say they have—well, what?—a tremendous crush on you? Something like that, anyway. . . . that's it, I guess. A crush—at least that, maybe more—I don't know."

He finally regained a trace of composure. "Well, Carol, there is probably some unfinished work for us to do. This kind of thing sometimes happens in treatment and can be worked out."

"I knew you'd say something like that. Anyway, I expected you to tell me that I was transferring—isn't that the word?— drawn to you by mistake, when really it was my father or someone like that. Now, listen to me. I may be misguided in my feelings, but I do know the feelings. They're real, they're very strong . . . and I hope you won't laugh at me."

"I'm not laughing," he replied, feeling helpless and embarrassed, but also vaguely excited. "What do you expect me to do?"

Carol became silent but finally did sit down. Her eyes cautiously left him and wandered, without focus, about the room. He remembered the curve of her neck, the firm lines of her face, and the natural softness of her mouth, all poised as if concentrated on selecting very carefully the next words she would speak.

"I've thought a lot about that," she began slowly. "I would like to meet you socially, outside the office, I mean."

"That's impossible," he replied reflexively and defensively.

"I know it's a crazy request when you first think about it. But then, why shouldn't we? I mean, I'm no longer your patient. We could at least become friends, get to know each other as people. That doesn't sound so dangerous does it?

"But. . . ." he could not summon the words, the rebuttal that he knew should have lain at his fingertips. How often he had heard supervisors offer just the right phrase for these classical moments of confrontation in psychotherapy. Such as when a homosexual patient expresses affection. One had suggested, "You might say 'I take your statement to mean that you and I can work together.' " Simple, direct, supportive, completely devoid of seduction. My god, dear supervisor, where are you now? Relax, it will come, he prayed.

But it did not come. He opened his mouth as if to reply,

but no words followed, certainly no right words, no solid, professional parry. What did come was an impulse to let go, to play it by ear, simply to see where Carol's suggestion would lead. He knew that he was beyond making choices, like a climber stranded on a perilous slope, suddenly conscious that he will inevitably lose his balance and fall, who decides to relax and sustain the impact as best he can.

"What did you have in mind?" he asked, almost with resignation.

"I've upset you, I can see that," Carol replied, somewhat ashamed but sympathetic.

"No, not really. What would you suggest?"

"Oh, I don't know, maybe a drink some evening after you have finished work here. Maybe at the Four Horsemen, you know, that little bar on South Main Street down by the river. They're open rather late, I think."

He decided to take the initiative. He had abandoned his professional role, sure enough. But at least he could be forthright. "What about, say, next Tuesday at ten-thirty."

"That would be fine," Carol quickly closed the negotiation, then gently added, "I hope you are not too upset. I promise not to rape you," she added teasingly yet tastelessly, she worried later, when she replayed the scene again and again in her mind.

Carol stood up and moved toward him as he by habit rose from his chair. She placed her left hand gently behind his neck and kissed him lightly, just at the outer margin of his lips, then quickly walked out of the office.

Following this meeting with Carol Smythe, his days became a curious mixture of pain and joy. Routines were negotiated almost without thinking, and his capacity for mindless stereotypy surprised and troubled him. Can so much of what I do each day require so little of me? he wondered. He wrote orders, progress notes, conducted group meetings, met with supervisors—all of this made up a separate, satellite sphere of his life, enlivened and sometimes perturbed by the shadowy awareness of his upcoming appointment. He perceived a curious buoyancy in himself and realized that he now had something to anticipate. The future, like a watered flower, was coming back to life. How long had it been, he pondered, since he had looked ahead with anything like a sense of excitement?

On the other hand, his individual work clearly suffered. When he was alone with a patient, trying to be for a time available to another's message, state of mind, problem—though he brought himself back time and again—there were persistent difficulties with concentration. Carol's face intruded again and again, with almost ghostly persistence. He finally gave up his attempts to banish thoughts of her and, as in their previous meeting, decided to go with the experience. He was first besieged, then overrun by erotic fantasies. She was confessing her love, he was undressing her, they were making love—in a car, in a forest, on a seashore, by a lake in moonlight. "My god, what romantic tripe," he berated himself, but the images returned, always returned. "How intriguing that I can listen for nearly an hour and scarcely remember a thing," he confessed privately, and recalled that Plato had compared erotic love to insanity, but never to dementia.

"And I don't really know what I'm going to do, Doctor," the man said. "You know that Esther and I have been estranged in our marriage for years. But I never thought it would come to this. I've been swept off my feet by another woman. What can I say? I never believed in this sort of thing. To me, marriage is forever. You take the good and the bad, don't you agree? . . . you do agree, don't you?"

"Agree? . . . Oh, yes, yes, of course. A very complex situation, Arturo, very complex . . . but I certainly can see the point you're making, the way you are thinking it through."

He was trying to listen, with little success, to Arturo Canelli, a 42-year-old businessman, a thoughtful, sensitive, yet unassertive man who had been reared in an anxiety-ridden household, tyrannized by an alcoholic father. Though timid, Arturo was scrupulous and industrious and had been able, without a high school education, to establish and maintain a very successful wholesale fruit business. One of his sons had tried to cheat him after Arturo had set the youngster up in a section of his business, and the resulting disillusionment had precipitated a depression that caused him to seek treatment. Arturo's wife was a rather plain but accommodating woman, severely inhibited sexually but a capable mother and wife in all other respects. She and Arturo had tacitly agreed to set the issue of sex aside rather than to continue their painful reciprocity of engagement and withdrawal, always out of phase. As he began to emerge from his depression, or perhaps even coincident with his improvement, Arturo began to talk about his life's hopes and disappointments. In the context of these discussions, he began to have fantasies of an affair with a secretary in one of his outlet stores. He vacillated back and forth in his session—should he act on his fantasy or shouldn't he? Arturo had been going on in this fashion for nearly half an hour, and he had simply not been listening. He and Carol were a rhythmic mass of tangled limbs, entwined on the floor of her apartment. Clearing his throat and shaking his head, he was able to bring Arturo back into focus.

"Do you believe in affairs, Doctor?" Arturo put the question bluntly.

He hesitated, like a man who considered for a moment that his mind had been read. "Believe in affairs? How do you mean that, Arturo?"

"You know, is it right? I mean can it ever be justified?"

"That's a difficult question; also too general. Maybe we should look at it from your perspective. I guess I believe a person has to think through and be ready to accept the consequences of his acts."

"Yeah, I agree. What would they be for me? The consequences . . . I don't know. If Rosa ever found out, she'd probably die. That is, she'd just never speak to me again. You know how she can freeze me out. I wonder if I'd be tempted to tell her?"

"You might want to tell her in order to handle your guilt?"

"Yes, probably. I have a hunch that would not be fair, though."

"Hardly. If you decide to have an affair you have to be able to manage the feelings involved."

"And how would I know ahead of time? . . . Guess there's no way of getting around an element of risk, is there?"

"Probably not."

"But, god, how wonderful it would be to have a woman love me again. Love my body, you know, love to touch me, lie next to me and be content. I've been a good husband to Rosa, but I can't remember when—if ever—she loved me like that. A man needs that, don't you think?"

"Yes. Most men do."

"Well, I could go on forever like this. . . . I guess I'll just have to make a decision, won't I?"

"I guess there's no other way."

Following his conversation with Carol, he had regained a degree of perspective and self-control. He rationalized the social meeting with a recently terminated patient as unusual, even possibly ill-advised, but not necessarily unethical, and beyond that he would take it as it came. If Carol seemed clearly unable to modulate her wish to be more involved with him, then he would simply refer her to someone else to work through the termination issue. It was a bit embarrassing, of course, that they had not managed a reasonable termination in the course of their sessions. He had some degree of insight into his push for a hurried end to the work and into his vulnerability to Carol's idealization of him. Somehow, after a little distance and much thought, he concluded that he had made a mistake but not a serious one. Without intending it, he had developed a series of inward responses to his own questions about the whole episode and would practice interrogating himself, like a religious youth might approach an occasion of sin armed with a few lines of catechism, hastily committed to memory.

Having arrived early, he was reassuring himself in this manner when he saw Carol appear at the doorway and nod in his direction after greeting the hostess. He watched as she approached through the mazelike aisles created by patternless tables and chairs. The bar was about half full, and the passageways between tables were narrowed, forcing Carol to rise to her toes and twist her hips alternately as she approached. He was certainly aware that the subtle movements with which she negotiated her way toward him were unplanned, yet she seemed to be saying, "Here I am. Watch me move, watch me as I come toward you. Watch my mouth and lips as I greet you. . . . Say no to me if you can, if you must, but first look at me and speak with me. . . ." He stood up slowly as she approached.

"Hello," Carol began with tactful hesitancy before glancing down as he helped her adjust her chair. "You been waiting long?"

"No . . . not really, a few minutes maybe," he replied, taking a seat closer than directly across the small, oval, wooden table, but not as close as he might have. Then he looked at her slowly and entirely. She was wearing a very light print dress with thin shoulder straps, which fit snugly above the waist and gathered loosely, without much bulk below. It seemed to be a light blue but he could not be certain in the dim light. She wore no jewelry except for very delicate gold pendant earrings that now and then caught the light and glittered brilliantly. Her hair, darker and longer than he had remembered, fell abundantly about her bare shoulders.

"Well, do you approve?" she teased, knowing that he did.

"You look lovely," he conceded, almost sadly.

She picked up his tone immediately and countered, "You sound rather disappointed. Now look, why don't we just relax and enjoy ourselves . . . I can tell you're tense. Maybe I am, too, to be honest, I'm very excited . . . just to be here with you—a chance to meet you in a different place, in a different way . . . okay?"

He felt curiously relieved by her openness, her honesty.

"You're right, you know, there's really no reason to be up-tight," he responded, remembering his prior self-examination and exoneration.

"Now," she began, as if she were chairing a committee meeting, "let me learn a little about you. So far it has been very one-sided. You know practically everything about me, and I know nothing about you. Except, of course, what I can guess . . . from simply looking. . . . Let me see, you're about 35 . . . married, any children?"

"Thirty-four actually, married, yes, and a son nearly 7 months old. His name is Sam, we call him Sammy . . . his grand-father is Sam also."

"Your father?"

"No, Elaine's—my wife's father."

"So your wife is Elaine. How long have you been married?"

"A little over 5 years—no, 4, yes, that's right."

"May I ask you something?" Carol replied impetuously.

"Sure, go ahead."

"What did you tell Elaine about tonight?"

"Nothing, really, I mean . . . well, you see, she's away, visiting her parents."

After giving their orders, both seemed to agree, without actually speaking, upon a period of silence. He turned slightly toward the large screened window and stared out toward the river. She followed his gaze, and they both sat watching the open space between the trees, the site of an old ferry landing. It was an evening for which summer is named. The breeze from the river bore a faint but distinct odor of riverbank and old, rotting, creosoted timbers. Nearer at hand, rampant honeysuckle claimed the air whenever the pulse of the river breeze ebbed. Now and then a cabin boat passed through the treeless stage and disappeared in the night downriver. Peepers still chorused along the water's edge, forming a backdrop to the hum of conversation inside the bar.

He was suddenly very grateful for this moment in his life, for some combination of Carol's expectant presence and the transcendent softness of the evening filled him with a childlike thanksgiving. He realized that the distance, the formality could not continue. He wanted desperately to be with this person.

They talked for more than 2 hours and she was just what he needed her to be—there, attentive, willing to listen.

"So now you know about me also," he concluded resignedly.

"I'm glad we were able to meet like this."

Unburdened, almost buoyant, he suggested they go for a walk along the river, and she was quickly at his side as he rose from the table. There was a path of sorts beside the riverbank that wound in and about the maple groves along the river's edge, marked here and there by old wooden benches badly in need of fresh paint. They walked slowly upriver from the illuminated area in front of the bar. At first he held her hand, then as the way darkened among the trees he placed his arm around her waist and drew her nearer. She responded by grasping him firmly with her free arm, and as they continued slowly along the path he became aware of the effortless unison of their movement. He felt almost yoked to her, yet found their union no impediment, and wondered why he did not feel guilty, then quickly banished the task of attempting to understand his joyfulness.

Two weeks later, when they met for coffee at his request, their faces spoke reluctance, sadness, and resolve, which each perceived quite clearly and with relief.

"Guess what," Carol began rhetorically, answering with her next breath. "I've gotten a job."

"Why that's wonderful. Tell me about it."

"I'm going to be doing art therapy with retarded adults at a day care center near home. Really excited about it." She nodded as she spoke, as if to emphasize her determination.

"You won't believe what I've decided," he countered. "I'm going to try to write a book."

"You are, seriously?" Carol responded with that tone of confident admiration which made him tremble.

"I've wanted to do it for quite a while now—write a history of the state hospital movement. I think it's timely; should be a nice balance to my clinical work. I guess I'll be spending all my spare time in the library."

Carol caught his meaning and answered back, "Yes, with the job now I'm really going to be stretched, too."

They held their steaming mugs of coffee with both hands and stared at some neutral point near the center of the table.

"Carol," he started slowly. She did not look up.

"I can't begin to tell you what a boost you've been for me. . . . I'm not too proud of myself, you know. I've felt bad . . . wondered why I agreed to meet you. . . . If you need some more treatment time, I can refer—"

She interrupted, "You've nothing to be ashamed of. I was as responsible as you were, and I could sense your reluctance all along . . . I think I need something to get into, really, and I believe the job may do it. You've been a boost for me too, you know."

He heard the unmistakable resolve in her voice, the inflection one learns to listen for and to rely upon, and he counted himself a very fortunate man.

RANDY: WHO TAUGHT AND WHO REMEMBERED HIS TEACHERS

Randolph T. Tomlinson, unlike many of his psychiatric colleagues, was completely at ease among other physicians. The reasons for his comfort had little to do with his own views about psychiatry and its proper place within or without the orbit of traditional medicine. In fact during 30 years of helping troubled people he had thought of himself as a doctor, had taken pride, when opportunities arose, to mention his 1 year each of residency in neurology and neurosurgery before changing to psychiatry. At such times he would say something like, "You know, I cracked heads and tapped knees for 2 years. But I really wasn't good with my hands so I went into psychiatry." One usually got the feeling that he saw this outcome of his training as a distinct compromise, this having to settle for psychiatry.

In 30 years of totally devoted and discreet professional work, he had learned so much that was generally unknown that he walked about like a priest, beloved and feared because of what he had been told by others in moments of despair. Unlike the priests, however he rarely had a clear answer. His capacity to comfort did not come mainly from his psychological acumen. He was simply dogged, persistently available. He waited trouble out. There was no tragedy, revelation, or personal pain that evoked surprise or dismay in him. He had heard so much that his characteristic lack of surprise by itself was soothing. Often troubled consultees waited to confirm their sense of hopelessness in his response, but they never could. That was often just the thread of support they needed to find the courage to look at a problem. He never said what specifically he thought it was that helped in his work with patients. He did not have much training in psychotherapy, or so it seemed. He did often talk of making a relationship, but never said much more.

He had personally lived through many changes in a medical specialty that is still in the process of evolving. His first position following training had been in a small, upstate private hospital where he and a young emigrant German psychiatrist, Erica Steurmer, had taken care of a clientele of upper-class Bostonians whose families valued the seclusion and secrecy of the setting. Keyhouse had once been a famous country inn at the turn of the century. Families would make the 2-hour coach ride on Sundays after church and enjoy a magnificent dinner served formally in the great front room. After dinner the children could explore the nearby forest and gather wild strawberries while their parents conversed in the shade of towering maples. Such settings seem to have their cycles, their seasons of growth and decay, like all living things. It is not certain what brought on the decline of the great, manorial country inns; perhaps the automobile or the passing of a gentler pace of living. Whatever it was, Keyhouse closed its doors as a Sunday destination in the late 1920's and lay fallow, its great lawns untended, for over 10 years. In time Hans Umbarger, a Boston physician, came upon it during his search for a site for a private psychiatric hospital. Umbarger was a devotee of what were then the newly publicized insulin treatments, and Keyhouse became what was derisively known as an insulin emporium. The formal dining hall was transformed into the recovery room for patients emerging from insulin coma, an early treatment for severe depressions and psychotic states. The after-dinner smoking and music room was renovated and equipped with large, porcelain tubs for the administration of cold baths, a balm for less severe excited conditions.

Randy Tomlinson and Erica Steurmer together directed treatment for the entire hospital, with the aid of nurses and a number of rather burly attendants. Erica's husband Franz had suffered a severe depression when the couple first emigrated from Germany, and despite several courses of electric-shock treatments he remained therafter a stunned, defeated man. Though he shared with Erica a cottage on the grounds at Keyhouse, Franz rarely emerged during the daytime. However, at night he became more active and sometimes took long walks alone, often not returning until after midnight. One night he did not return at all and was found the following morning, hanging from a heavy limb by a crudely improvised noose. The suicide had taken place within easy view of the front door of Franz and Erica's cottage.

Randy and Erica became lovers long before Franz's suicide. It was almost inevitable because they worked side-by-side 12 hours a day, which began at 7 a.m. when they made the rounds of the entire hospital. The census usually included about 50 patients, of whom approximately one-half were receiving insulin or electric-shock treatment at a given time. After rounds, Randy would administer the insulin to designated patients at staggered intervals, and Erica would monitor the progress of coma induction in the large treatment room. She learned to begin the glucose injections at just the right time to allow for rapid emergence from the hypoglycemic state. In contrast to most practitioners who had used insulin extensively, she never lost a patient to irreversible coma. After the insulin treatments had been completed for the day, Erica and Randy together administered the electric shock. Patients were brought one at a time into the treatment room and placed on a padded, wooden table. Attendants immobilized each arm and leg against the cushioned surface, for the force of an unmodified convulsion could cause spinal fractures if the patients were not held down firmly. Even then, fractures sometimes occurred. Randy manned the shock machine and Erica monitored the patient's pulse, blood pressure, and breathing. Delivering patient after patient to this kind of physiological brink, then rescuing them, left both Randy and Erica emotionally denervated by about 1 p.m. each day. She had been the first to suggest that they have lunch together. Thereafter, they would often pack a picnic basket and hike off into the woods to dissipate the tension built up from the morning's work.

Erica Steurmer did not look like a German physician. To begin with, she was slender, with long, graceful arms. When she bent over a patient at the bedside, her abundant auburn hair fell across her face, which was more oval than round. Her features were delicate, even childlike, and she spoke regularly in a near whisper. One thing about her was true to her heritage, however, and that was her professional manner. She was deadly serious about her work and abided no sloppiness or casualness in the hospital staff. Her soft voice could convey the fierceness of a field marshal if she felt a patient's condition were being taken lightly. Randy admired this quality immensely, for it was this feeling about taking care of patients that he shared with her. Erica never spoke to Randy about Franz.

They made love on their first picnic together, and Erica had been the initiator of their intimacy. Randy had been totally surprised at her forwardness, yet their union seemed natural to him. They had been talking about a patient who was not responding to treatment, a young schizophrenic man who had been to Keyhouse twice before. Both were filled with the hopelessness of the young man's condition when Erica simply leaned toward Randy and kissed him softly. Their first lovemaking seemed to derive its intensity from a silent sharing of their knowledge of the young patient's ultimate fate. Randy always felt that their affair was an act of hopeful defiance, a symbolic ritual of stewardship wherein he and Erica tried to kindle life and love while all around them, in the suffering of their patients, hope seemed to be slipping away.

Following Franz Steurmer's suicide, Erica went away alone for a month. She refused to tell Randy where she was going, yet he perceived that she was struggling with guilt of great and expanding proportions. Somehow, so long as Franz was alive and she was essentially nursing him, Erica could allow herself the pleasure of the love affair with Randy. She had even brought herself finally to believe that Franz knew about the affair and condoned it because of his own incapacity and Erica's willingness to remain with him and take care of him. He was chronically suicidal; both Randy and Erica acknowledged that, but they also knew well that he had lived in that withdrawn, morose state for over 3 years at Keyhouse without making an actual attempt to end his life. The fact and manner of the suicide destroyed the fantasy that both Erica and Randy maintained. Franz must have known about their relationship and planned his suicide as one final, self-disclosing statement of bitterness and revenge. And his act did have the effect he must have desired; it drove Erica and Randy irrevocably apart.

When she returned from her trip, she let it be known in her quiet, resolute manner, that their affair was ended. Randy had never actually fallen in love with her, though he felt he might have, in time, if the circumstances of their working together could have changed. They clung to each other at Keyhouse like two battlefield surgeons, their relationship charged with an intensity that flowed fundamentally from a shared and powerful experience. They had never found an opportunity to be together, away from Keyhouse, to test the naturalness of their affection for one another.

Nevertheless, Randy was deeply upset by Erica's decision, for he soon rediscovered that her love quite literally gave him the strength to endure the agony of Keyhouse. Hopelessness, petulance, blind fury, dementia, madness—all were tolerable in the context of her presence and her love. Without her, the full, unmodified force of these furies, gathered and concentrated at Keyhouse, bore down upon him. The insulin coma became a devious, barbaric assault upon the energy system of the brain. The electric-shock treatments seemed like ludicrous, ungainly blows to the head, prompted mainly by frustration and impatience. Randy began to hate to see the sun rise at Keyhouse, for he had lost his capacity to keep hope alive, for himself and his patients. He knew that he would have to leave, that he could not continue in that setting without Erica. For her part, Erica became even more attached to Keyhouse, some said cloistered there, and she directed Umbarger's hospital for fifteen more years before a second marriage to a wealthy art collector who had once been a grateful recipient of her gentle and resolute physicianship at the old converted inn.

Randy had noted the subtle changes for months, perhaps for nearly a year, but had largely ignored them, for he nurtured a faith in his own longevity which was almost unshakable. His father, 92 years old, could still read the large-print version of the *New York Times* and bend your ear for an hour or so afterward. When Randy visited him at the nursing home, the old man would be in his room, bow tie affixed, listening to music or regaling the nurses with the early history of the town. His father still called him Junior; it was enough to make a man feel certain assurances about his own old age.

Yet he could clearly recall an October morning, almost a year before. A Saturday it was, and he had gotten up at 7 a.m. as usual. Breakfast was as usual—toast, unsweetened grapefruit juice, and black coffee. He would walk the mile to the post office and back before driving to his crosstown office to see two or three patients before noon. A classic fall morning greeted him, and the village was vintage New England. The maples were startling, flaming oranges and reds, the air so crisp one wanted to suck it in, to taste it between lips and tongue. The river was visible a mile or so to the south, a blue-gray track bordered by willows that remained unaltered by the mysterious chemistry that had recently wrought such wonder in the broader leaves. Halfway to the post office he noticed it—a strange, dull ache in his right calf. Stopping to adjust his socks, thinking they might be too tight, he noticed that the ache diminished momentarily. He then proceeded toward the post office, instictively walking more slowly, and after 100 yards or so felt the unfamiliar gripping pain again.

Claudication. That was the word Stanley Pinkerton, his internist, had used the following Monday. And that was not all: His electrocardiogram revealed an atrial arrhythmia with a ventricular rate of 110. Pinkerton had suggested he take a vasodilator as well as digoxin, and he had done so for about a month with good results. The calf pain rarely recurred, though he also walked less often. After a month he stopped taking the vasodilator but continued the digoxin, reasoning that it was not so ominous for a man of 65 to take a dose of Withering's remedy once a day. By reducing his walking he was able to avoid the claudication except for an occasional twinge. Thus did he relegate the early warnings of arterial disease to some small corner of his mind. It was several months later, after an episode of dizziness and transient confusion, that he began to grasp the extent of the disorder. He then did a rather curious thing—though in retrospect it was typical of him—he contacted a distinguished neuropsychologist in Boston and talked him into doing a full battery of tests. If his faculties were failing, he wanted to know precisely how and to what degree.

The report was unequivocal, but Randy had expected it. One hand had felt particularly clumsy on the pegboard. The test required that he match wooden pieces of various shapes with their appropriate slots while blindfolded. The left hand had gone all right but the shapes of the blocks did not seem definite when he tried it with his right hand. He also lost his sequences several times on the test that required him to draw a line connecting consecutive series of numbers and letters: A-1-B-2-C-3, and so forth.

"This elderly gentleman shows some evidence of decline in functions which depend upon the parietal association areas, particularly on the left side. Test impairment is spotty and suggests patches of neuronal deficit rather than broad areas of degeneration. . . ." So read the crux of the report that Randy had insisted be sent to him. Gratuitously, the neuropsychologist went on to make some specific suggestions: "In the light of these findings it would be advisable that this gentleman begin to consider curtailing the extent of his professional commitments. . . ."

A recommendation that he retire was much more than Randy had anticipated. It was true that occasionally he forgot the names of patients and sometimes even found it difficult to call to mind just the right words when composing a letter. He always took great pride in his consultation reports and was a master at communicating his findings and suggestions to another physician. His letters conveyed the thoroughness of his evaluations and the thoughtfulness of his advice. As some individuals give serious attention to dress, Randy regarded his professional correspondence as the most obvious and most lasting reflection of himself. For him a good consultation note was almost a sacred trust. In the loss of that elegant subtlety, he first confronted the seriousness of the arteriosclerotic process.

> There is at least one consolation: The past has become so vivid. I can hardly remember my phone number or the day of the week, but those days in Stockbridge are now as clear as a dream. And good days they were too. After Keyhouse, especially, and Erica. I will never forget the day I left. I see her now, walking me to my old Chevy coupe. How I ever got the trunk to stay on top I'll never know. Steady as a mountain pack it rode, though. She told me I should understand that she had to stay at Keyhouse. What eyes! I think she still loved me even then. I broke down, couldn't stop crying till I got to Worcester. Then the snow began outside Westfield and my windshield wipers caked up, took me five more hours to get to Lee. But by then I knew I was going to be all right. Still another hour to Stockbridge, making no more than five miles an hour. And he was there waiting—Riggs himself, looking like some kind of mountain man, walking slowly out to the car as I pulled in. "Dr. Tomlinson," he said, "welcome to The Austen Riggs Institute . . . and to winter in the Berkshires." The place reminded me very much of Keyhouse at first. The fire, blazing away and the old man standing before it, hands behind his back, giving me the history of the place. All I could think about was getting warm. I was hungry . . . but I listened . . . or tried to, while he rambled on and on.
>
> Riggs was originally an internist, carriage trade type who treated so many neurotics that he decided to start a special kind of hospital. Believed that people needed to get away, learn new habits. That was it—change their ways, de-

velop disciplines. He used to talk to his patients in groups, sit 'em down like they were in school. Tell 'em about their minds, he did, slipping in a little Freud here and there, with a special New England twist. I still have his *Talks to Patients*. "You see, Randy"—I remember he called me Randy right away—"You see, Randy we're trying to do something different here. Now I know about Keyhouse, the shock treatments and the insulin and all. We don't do that. We mainly give our patients time, time to think about their lives. We help them, too, starting right from the beginning. Old Adolf Meyer was right, all of a person's life is important, and we go through it bit by bit, looking for patterns. You don't have to say much when you really get a person going about their life. It's the most important thing to all of us, but you've got to put people at ease, let them know you aren't going to judge, listen them out."

I never knew anyone who treated individual lives with such gentleness as Riggs did. It is a bit outrageous, after all. A strange profession, preposterous, really. Maybe that is our foolhardy contribution, a kind of recklessness in the face of time, evolution, and all. "Listen," he used to say, "listen to the story of this life, listen to its artistry, its struggle, its triumph and its failure. Find a way to kindle hope." God, such presumption. In the long run what can it matter? I used to think that and sometimes say it, even to him. He would reply gently that perhaps I had not listened carefully enough. And then there were the talks. My god, I believe Riggs was a frustrated preacher. Those goddam things were deadly—tight as hell from a logical point of view, but more soporific than bromide. He'd come in smiling confidently— always upbeat he was—and say, "today, friends"—he always called the patients friends—"Today, friends," he'd say, "I'm going to talk to you about The Individual *or* Sensation and Emotion *or* The Problem of Adaptation. . . ." Can you imagine? The back row would begin to nod right after he'd announce the title. . . . I recall the day that manic fellow from Springfield . . . Charles . . . no, Chalmers . . . Chambers, I believe . . . the day he stood up and began to argue back: "Now, Dr. Riggs, you say some of us are overly sensitive, but what proof do you have? Take me, for instance, I've never had anything but trouble all my life, but I've mastered it, endured it at every turn. Why, I could give a lecture on endurance." And on and one he went; Riggs stood patiently and waited for a pause, and there weren't many, but when Chambers finally caught his breath, Riggs said, "Mr. Chambers, you may indeed lecture *after* I am through," and, by god, the fellow sat down and shut up.

Then there were the everlasting winters, snow like I had never seen before, falling, falling, and building up on huge drifts. The younger patients would spend hours making snow figures. I remember one of me, beard and all, looking fierce. Then the long walks in the woods when the snow was not too deep. Riggs thought long walks were good for you, probably something he learned from his TB work and just borrowed over into psychiatry. He used to lead us out on those cold, clear days. We'd start up the hill, the birches and the sun, so bright you would have to squint. About half staff and half patients, and we'd hike clear over to the lake which was frozen solid, make a fire, have some tea and sandwiches, and then head back. I can still see him, the woolen hat and heavy leather boots and the long red scarf. Sometimes we'd sing, too, and then the line of hikers would look like a little steam train, all puffing together. And finally, back in the main house, there was never anything as satisfying as the thawing out—birchwood smoke, steaming mittens, hot cider.

ELLEN: WHOSE ILLNESS FADES SLOWLY FROM MEMORY

Tom Grayson had been ecstatic when he met Martha Fulton 25 years before at the University of Colorado. She was different from the other girls he had known, unusually pretty but aloof, sensitive, interested in the arts. Tom had been a superb athlete and was extremely popular. His personality was a strict complement to Martha's, for he was as open as she was closed, as obvious as she was opaque. Their relationship began and persisted as a clear attraction of opposites. With him Martha felt wanted, secure, safely escorted through the complexities of college life, which she felt totally unable to manage alone. Tom was never anything but straightforward about his plans for the future. Since boyhood he had dreamed of being a gentleman rancher. He wanted a working place, somewhere in the foothills of the mountains where he could raise top-flight beef stock and try his luck with quarter horses on the side. He spoke of his plans openly with Martha, sensing the enormous differences between them and hoping to entice her into becoming part of his dream. She originally had hopes of becoming an actress or a dancer, for on the stage her social anxieties were swept aside. In performing, she felt completely at ease, as if the medium of the dance or the dramatic role were a disguise in which she could give herself over to spontaneity and freedom of expression. However, these early thrusts toward self-discovery were overcome by the force of her attraction to Tom Grayson. Ignoring the radical differences in their personalities, they both literally never looked back. Tom proposed on the day of graduation, and they were married the following fall. His father—a wealthy merchant in Pueblo—gave them the ranch in Trinidad as a wedding present. Martha was 6 months pregnant with Ellen on the anniversary of her graduation from college.

The first few months in Trinidad had been chaotic. The ranch house had required a thorough interior redecorating, which Martha had supervised with substantial taste and skill. Tom had thrown himself into the tasks of getting his herd started. He bought a bull, three heifers, and two working ponies. The barn was in relatively good shape, but most of the fence needed mending, and a small feeder lot had to be built. From 6 in the morning until late at night Tom Grayson worked like a man possessed. Though he had spent many summers working on different ranches in eastern Colorado, he found that owning a ranch was quite another matter. He spent endless hours seeking advice and assistance from his willing neighbors, who took a bemused pride in helping the energetic greenhorn who, with his pretty, shy bride, had come to live in their midst. The first winter was particularly severe, and the Graysons lost two of their first three calves. Still, the challenge of making their own way kept spirits high, and when Martha discovered she was pregnant, their sense of starting something together seemed even stronger.

As Tom drove he retraced the events surrounding Ellen's birth. It had been June, the month when the high meadows leap to life almost overnight. The pastureland flowers in myriad variety, the aspen leaf out, and the streams roll toward the flat land flushed by the first runoff from the eastern slope. It seemed the right time for human birth, a time when all of nature was coming alive. And the birth itself had been relatively easy. After a 6-hour labor, the only obstetrician in Trinidad, an easygoing elderly man named Adams, had given Martha a low spinal when she was 8 centimeters, and 30 minutes later Ellen had cried lustily. It was in the recollection of what came afterward that Tom's memory became laced with confusion and anxiety. Doc Adams had seemed vaguely perplexed. He first announced to Tom that he and Martha had a healthy 7-pound daughter, but, as Tom recalled, added as an aside that Martha seemed to be unusually exhausted. The exhaustion was indeed severe and out of keeping with the otherwise unremarkable delivery. Martha lay in bed, had no appetite, and seemed peculiarly uninterested in her newborn child. After 7 days, Doc Adams' composure changed and he told Tom that a psychiatric consultation was advisable. The only available psychiatrist was in Alamosa, a man named Jacobs. Tom recalled his meeting with Jacobs after the consultation with Martha.

"Your wife is severely depressed, Mr. Grayson. I think she needs to go to a hospital."

Tom Grayson simply did not comprehend what Jacobs had said. "But she's in a hospital now," he replied with astonishment.

"I mean she needs to go to a psychiatric hospital. There are no facilities here to treat her condition."

"I just don't know what you mean, Doc." Tom had searched for something familiar or at least comprehensible in Dr. Jacobs' recommendation.

"Mr. Grayson, your wife is suffering from a condition known as postpartum depression. It sometimes happens following childbirth. Has your wife had any prior mental problems?"

Tom was speechless. "I . . . I don't know . . . I mean, no, I don't think so. . . . Doc, are you sure? Let me talk to her. There must be some mistake. She has always been normal . . . I mean, you know, like other people. She was very excited about the baby

. . . I don't know, Doc. How can this happen?" Tom realized he was on the verge of panic or tears—probably both.

"Now, Mr. Grayson, there is no need for worry. In Denver there is a good hospital. A few shock treatments and she'll be as good as new."

It had all happened too fast. The trip to Denver, the admission to Colorado Psychopathic, Martha's seeming lack of concern for the whole process. The signing of the consent form for electric-shock treatments. Will they hurt? No of course not. She won't remember them. (Oh, God, what shall I do?) You must give your permission, Mr. Grayson, or we can't carry out the treatments. Yes . . . of course. (Oh my God, what is happening?) Martha, what shall we do? I don't know, Tom. Do what you think is best. . . . Is there any other treatment? No, none that we know of. Will there be any after effects? Just a little memory loss. Memory loss? How much, I mean will she forget everything? No, of course not, just recent things. Can she take care of the baby? Yes, certainly, in time. Now if you'll just sign here . . . (Oh my God, help us). . . .

Tom Grayson had stayed in Denver throughout the period of Martha's hospitalization. Each day when they brought her back from the treatment room he was there to watch her slow emergence from stupor, mumbling, thrashing, slowly coming around. After the fourth treatment she did not seem to recognize him at all for several minutes after she woke. He became used to the amnesia that lasted the better part of a day following the last six treatments. Slowly, between treatments, her personality began to return. She started to eat and to converse spontaneously with Tom and the nurses. She asked where she was, what had happened, how long she had been there. She remembered being pregnant but had no recollection of the delivery. After 4 weeks Martha and Tom returned to the ranch on a warm July afternoon.

Now, as he drove along the eastern outskirts of Denver toward the airport, Tom felt a tragic sense of déjà vu. It was happening all over again, he decided. The secret, the old, unspeakable secret had returned from banishment. Though he and Martha had successfully concealed her psychiatric history from

the children—even at considerable cost to their peace of mind—
it was now reemerging, reincarnate, in their daughter.

Nor did his first glimpse of Ellen relieve his anxiety. She
appeared at the exit portal looking gaunt and exhausted. One
of the flight attendants was carrying Little Tom. Tom Grayson
embraced his daughter without a word, yet his forcefulness surprised Ellen, and with this act he somehow broke free from the
tyrannical reverie that had dominated his thinking since he left
Trinidad.

"So glad to see you, dear! How was the trip? Was Little Tom
a good traveler? Here, let me take him. Thank you, ma'am, thank
you so much . . . that's a boy. Your grandaddy is here now . . .
now don't you worry about a thing."

Through the stale sameness of her mood Ellen was touched
by her father's welcome and began to cry softly.

"Now, baby, it's all right. Yes it is, now. You'll see. A little
rest here where the air is good . . . you'll see. Won't she, Tommy
boy? We'll take good care of Mommie, won't we, you and me.
Yes, sir."

The drive back to Trinidad was painful for them both. Tom
talked about his herd, the goodly number of yearlings they had
collected, how the market price of beef was on the rise. He rattled
on about David's last football season, that he was sure to be a
college star. He was fast, could cut on a dime, and could catch
anything thrown his way. Pretty good in school, too—nothing
flashy, but steady, a real hard worker. He would probably get
into the university easy enough, even had a crack at a football
scholarship. And Sarah, she was her mother's pride. She was in
the high school dramatics club, took singing lessons, and would
probably get the lead female part in the spring musical.

Ellen knew her father was anxious because he was making
small talk nonstop. She was relieved in a way, for casual conversation would have been a wretched burden in her current
frame of mind. It was as if nothing could hold her interest, so
that words only existed, as if in a dictionary, lists of colorless
things, names without referents, dispirited symbols without purchase in the world. She nodded occasionally, hoping that Tom
would continue his chatter. As she watched the countryside pass,
the oppression of her mood tore into her consciousness. "This

is the dawning of the year," she told herself, "there is hope and promise everywhere. Yet I am as desolate as midwinter. Will it ever end, or even lift for a while, this cloud, this crust upon my senses?"

"But enough of our doings. How about you? How are you feeling?" Tom had decided that he must ask, that he had to know if his fears were well founded.

Ellen knew she could not hide any longer. "I am not doing so well, Daddy. . . . I can't seem to shake this thing. Ever since Little Tom came—except for a few weeks there—I've been very down. I hate to burden you and Mother like this. But my doctor thought that a visit home might do some good."

"Of course it will, dear. You've probably just been working too hard. A mother has lots to do. It's not easy being a mother. Well, now. Let's not make too much of all this. I'm sure your mother will know how to perk you up. She's all set to help all she can."

Ellen doubted that her mother was all set for anything, recalling Martha's perfunctory visit after the birth, and how eager she had been to leave. Martha Grayson was many things, but she was neither supportive nor comforting to people in need. She could do for you but she could not feel with you.

"Dad, I think I'm going to need some professional help while I'm here." Ellen had come to this conclusion on the flight home. After the brief novelty of a change of scene had begun to fade, she had been seized by the realization that she would be emotionally alone.

"We'll get whatever you need, dear. Don't you worry about that." Tom realized he had no idea as to what he was promising, but he was determined that Ellen would never receive shock treatments. He was convinced that the treatments had permanently changed his wife in some subtle yet powerful way and felt guilty for having allowed them, for he had focused the blame for all of Martha's subsequent aloofness and resignation on the shock treatments themselves. This time he would not sign. There must be alternatives. Surely in 21 years there had been some progress made in the treatment of this condition. It would be different this time.

By mid-April the novelty of the homecoming had dissipated.

When Ellen and Little Tom first arrived in Trinidad their presence was casually explained as a routine trip home. The Graysons visited family friends, showed off their grandson, and assuaged their anxiety about Ellen's state of mind by keeping her busy. At first, this forced activity seemed to help. Toward the end of the day, at least, Ellen usually felt her mood and energy improve somewhat. Curiously, around supper time she would catch herself responding to some humorous comment her father had made or feel an upsurge of warmth and availability for Little Tom. At such times, she dared at first to hope that the process was burning itself out, that the inchoate, invisible dam that had long and capriciously held her feelings in check was at last giving way. Invariably, the following morning such hopes were overpowered by the return of the awful helplessness, the lethargy, wrapped in the insipid gray of the world she woke to find. She came to regard the evening respite as a cruel hoax, a sadistic trick of fate that seemed to lure her hopes from hiding and crush them. Though livelier toward evening, she finally refused to be buoyed by this interlude. At that point Tom Grayson knew it was time to get help.

Dr. Marc Jacobs, the first psychiatrist to practice in Alamosa and the one who had recommended hospitalization for Martha Grayson after Ellen's birth 23 years before, had begun to reduce his patient load. At age 62 he had decided not to take any new patients, though the decision was not yet widely known throughout the local medical community. Still, his was the only name Tom Grayson knew in connection with emotional difficulties.

Tom always acted as if his fearful brush with psychiatry years before had been forgotten, although he was aware that Martha still had sessions with Jacobs from time to time. In one sense, he resented that he had never been included, for he inwardly acknowledged the stalemate in their marriage that had developed gradually though inexorably over the years. Like the movement of the hands of a clock, the actual change in their relating would have been difficult to perceive at any one moment in their lives; yet the distances between them were unmistakable when viewed over time. At some point in the distant past Tom might have earnestly worked to improve the marriage, but not any longer. Whatever compromises the couple had made seemed relatively stable, so that in recent years he had almost managed to ignore Martha's occasional visits to Jacobs, just the way he ignored her trips to Denver and the opera. When Tom finally decided to call Jacobs, he was seized once again by the same anxiety that had first overwhelmed him upon Ellen's return. Still, he phoned.

"Hello, this is Dr. Jacobs." The tone was one of distinct weariness.

"Hello, Dr. Jacobs? This is Tom Grayson calling, from over in Trinidad. . . . My wife is a patient of yours, I think, yes . . . I know she is. . . . Hello, are you there, Doc?" Tom realized Jacobs had not yet signalled his recognition of the caller.

"Yes, sure, I'm here, Mr. Grayson. What can I do for you?" Jacobs said after an awkward pause, during which he had been reflexively considering the possible reasons for the call. Of course his first thought was that Martha Grayson was in trouble. God forbid, could it be a relapse or a suicide attempt? Unlikely after so many years . . . probably not. . . . No . . . Grayson wants to complain about the bill . . . but he never has before. Then what?

"Doc, I think my daughter needs your help . . . (another pause of several seconds) . . . I'm having trouble talking about this over the phone. Could I come over and see you?"

"Well, actually Mr. Grayson, I'm not taking any new patients now."

"Oh,'s that so. . . . You don't say. . . . Well, do you suppose you might just talk to Ellen and see . . . since my wife's been with you for so long and all . . . you know us pretty good, I reckon."

After another lengthy silence, Tom heard, "I guess I could see her and try to find out what the problem is. This is Ellen, is it?"

"That's right, Doc. She's home for a visit and a rest. Been pretty busy since her baby was born. Our first grandson, you know. Named him Tom after me. . . ."

"When can you bring her over?"

"Just anytime you say, Doc. Soon as possible."

"Would tomorrow at four be convenient?"

"We'll be there. Thanks so very much, Doc."

"Of course; see you then."

Ellen was almost startled when she stepped into Dr. Jacob's

consultation room in Alamosa. To begin with, the room was rather clumsily attached to his house, a very modern structure built flush against gray rock and surrounded by 10 or so acres of aspen and pine, nearly 2 miles west from the center of town. A fair-sized brook ran within 50 feet of the door and contributed that perpetual musical, gurgling sound, cheery enough during daylight but indistinguishable from rain at night. The brook, in its brief course along the westward rim of the lot, was largely hidden from view at ground level due to a high bank thrown up by earth movers to prevent water damage to the house during the annual spring runoff. At Jacob's property a headgate had been installed to regulate the downstream flow for a rather intricate network of irrigation channels that fed a large hayfield to the south and east.

The room they entered was distinctly Western. Two chairs, heavily wooded and Spanish in flavor, flanked a matching coffee table. The walls were decorated with framed photographs evidently taken by Jacobs himself, one of the nearby brook, bordered by gold and sun-streaked aspen in the fall. The other was shot at timberline, a rather stunning piece that focused upon a gnarled scrub cedar stump set against a luminous sunset with mountains for a background.

Tom and Ellen were not sure whether the room they had entered was a waiting room or a consultation room. As they searched for some clue, Jacobs entered from a door that led to the interior of the house. Through the door a modestly furnished living room was visible.

"Good morning. I see you found your way alright," Dr. Jacobs greeted them.

"Sure thing, Doc. Good directions, real good," Tom Grayson replied, looking sharply at Ellen and back again to Jacobs, as if trying to establish some connection between them with the sweep of his gaze. "Dr Jacobs, I'd like you to meet my oldest daughter, Ellen. . . . Ellen, Dr. Jacobs."

"How do you do, Ellen," Jacobs replied warmly. Ellen smiled and nodded to his greeting but did not actually speak. Jacobs sensed her sadness instantly—the set expression on her face suggesting apathy as much as pain, the subtle inattention to grooming, the shoulders slumped, bearing an invisible weight. For a brief moment no one spoke, as if a cue had been missed, but then Dr. Jacobs began.

"I . . . I'm not sure if you want your father to join us, Ellen . . . or—"

"Tom broke in, "Oh no, Doc, you and Ellen go right ahead. I can just wait outside. That'll be fine for me. . . ."

"I'm afraid," Jacobs began apologetically, "that I don't have a separate waiting room. As I mentioned, I've been cutting down on my practice. I closed my office in town and added this room to the house. . . . You are welcome to wait in the living room here."

"That's okay, Doc. I'll just take a little walk outside—you and Ellen go ahead." Tom opened the door as he spoke and made it clear that he preferred the freedom to move around over the invitation to sit in the living room of a strange house. "You just signal when you're done here. I'll be around close by." With an overly confident air, he closed the door gently and left.

Ellen had been carefully observing Marc Jacobs during this exchange. He was nearly six feet tall with a deeply-lined face that radiated gentleness. His informal manner was accentuated by long, rather unruly gray hair. He wore dark slacks and a flannel shirt buttoned at the neck. A thin string tie was secured at the neck by a small silver ringlet, probably Indian silverwork, Ellen guessed. She felt at ease with him and sat down in one of the sturdy chairs without hesitation.

Jacobs could see the resemblance to Martha Grayson. Ellen was taller than her mother, but her forehead and expressive mouth were clearly theirs in common. And the subtle grace as she moved, this too reminded him of Martha. But there was no mistaking the depression; unfortunately they clearly bore a similar burden.

"Now, Ellen," Dr. Jacobs began, "tell me about your trouble."

Ellen took a long breath, as if preparing a complicated, tiresome account. "This all began with the birth of my son, several months ago. Following the delivery I was very tired, exhausted, really. At first I thought that I was just having trouble getting my strength back. After a few weeks, though, I knew it was more than that. I began to lose interest in the baby—Tommy is his name, after my father, of course. I lost my appetite and my energy just went flat. Everything I tried to do was a big chore. I was tired all day but couldn't sleep at night either.

Ellen paused to see if Dr. Jacobs wanted to question her, then proceeded after sensing that he was still listening. "Then one day I rather impulsively brought up to my husband the possibility of going home. . . . I don't know why I thought of it. . . . I guess I was feeling lonely and frustrated by my lack of progress. The idea of being at home, with family to look after me . . . it just came to mind. Then to my surprise my husband picked right up on my suggestion and before I realized it, plans were being made."

Since coming home to Colorado, Ellen had tried gamely to hold her deepest despair in check. Though weighted down continuously with the burden of her depression, she had learned to shoulder it each day and to bear it with a certain dignity and silence. A fragile stalemate existed between the unrelenting pressure of her mood and her own inner strength, which seemed to arise from a source deeper than her sadness. This strength was never robust enough to overcome the depression for any period of time; it was one of those valiant rearguard actions of our lives that go forth to oppose unfriendly forces that we know will one day be victorious. However, now in Dr. Jacob's office she was suddenly overpowered by an urge to let go, to withdraw from the field. She could no longer resist. Her decision, though it was not really a decision in the usual sense, was signalled only by a sudden stiffening of her expression, a tonic clenching of her jaw, and the coursing of a narrow wash of tears down both cheeks. It was neither a vivid nor a dramatic moment, unless one observed with a practiced eye.

Marc Jacobs sensed from the beginning that Ellen was suffering from a significant depression. The very fact that she was Martha's daughter immediately put her into a special category. For he knew Martha Grayson's depression as well as he knew anything or anyone in his entire professional career. He had agreed to see Martha after her hospitalization and shock treatments years ago. The intervening years were telescoped in his memory; yet he knew that the intricacies of his work with her were meticulously recorded in a record at least half an inch thick that was filed in the adjoining room. He thought of the record, the notes in different colors of ink but always in his own handwriting, as if by a fantasied scanning of his progress notes he could enliven Martha's patienthood. Those records bespoke a certain professional fidelity that the two of them had created over the years. They had developed a way of working together that seemed good enough to sustain Martha through the isolated years on the farm, through her disappointment in herself for having abandoned a promising vocation, and through her bitterness at Tom's repeated emotional and physical withdrawal. Not that Jacobs had seen her frequently, either, though initially they did meet once a week. Following her hospitalization, the meetings were just about that frequent for almost a year. During this period Marc Jacobs felt that substantial progress had been made. Martha had come to recognize her idealization of Tom, her willingness to ignore some relatively obvious negative traits— such as his basic mistrust of people—in order to belong to and be protected by him. Jacobs had basically helped Martha—a sheltered, inexperienced, young married woman—emerge into and tolerate the shocks of early and middle adulthood. After the first year or so she would return rather irregularly, sometimes for a single visit, sometimes for a series of sessions lasting several months. She herself would initiate each reinstitution and termination of treatment, and Jacobs had learned to trust her instincts completely.

In the early 1960s Jacobs found that some of the new medication for depression was helpful for Martha. Whereas before he had endured with her the symptomatic cycle of her depressions, with the medication such symptoms as insomnia, lack of energy, decline in usual interests, and difficulty in concentration were fairly rapidly attenuated, and it became possible to focus more quickly on the clashes between Martha and the world she perceived, which almost invariably lay behind each new symptomatic relapse. On occasion she even seemed to get a bit overstimulated by the medication. At these times, Jacobs recalled almost humorously, she became a rather different person, somewhat to Tom's chargin, and would be more openly assertive, more responsive and innovative sexually, and a bit freer with her money. Judicious reductions in the medication always kept these episodes under control, yet Jacobs had always suspected that Martha's nervous system was capable of generating a full manic attack under certain circumstances.

So now we have Martha's daughter, looking very much like her mother, sounding very much like her, he concluded. This is likely a significant depression, with the clear family history to underscore it. Twenty years ago she would probably have required hospitalization. We may be able to avoid that now, if we are fortunate with the medication. I wonder if she could overshoot? Well, I can worry about that if it comes up.

Jacobs tried to respond to his sense that Ellen had temporarily given into her hopelessness. "You've been trying to manage this pretty much alone, I take it?"

Without looking up, she nodded in a way that confirmed his impression. "I've wanted to spare Mom and Dad in this . . . but I can't cope by myself anymore."

"I'm glad you came," Jacobs chose his words carefully. "As you know, your mother and I have worked together over the years with good success."

At first, Jacob's words passed over Ellen almost unnoticed. When depressed, she found herself sorting through conversation much as one might sort through old clothes, absent-mindedly and without much attention or interest. However, something Jacobs said pierced the too-familiar dullness.

"What did you say?" Ellen asked almost perfunctorily.

Suddenly Jacobs realized that it was quite possible that Martha's psychiatric history was completely unknown to her daughter. In fact, judging from the blank surprise on Ellen's face it now seemed likely. He chastised himself for not considering the possibility before. Certainly nothing that Tom had said suggested a confidence that the family wanted maintained, he rationalized. Anyway, there was no option now.

"I have treated your mother quite successfully on and off for a number of years," Jacobs tried to sound steady and professional, adding, "I'm a bit surprised that you weren't aware of it."

"I'm surprised too," Ellen managed to murmur, almost too stunned to respond, focusing on the photograph of scrub cedar. She was out there for a moment, a part of the misshapen wood at the edge of growing things, its aesthetic force intricately linked to a struggle for survival. She seemed to be processing the new information, as if a critical integer or pattern were suddenly discovered missing from a life program of many years, so that her own instinctive image of herself would now have to wait upon a restructuring of the past with the new knowledge in place. She appeared, in the midst of her depressive state, unable to assimilate Jacob's revelation. She muttered almost too softly for Jacobs to hear.

"You treated my mother . . . for years . . . we never knew . . . but when did she come? . . . But of course . . . but why didn't they tell me? . . . Daddy must have known. . . . then why didn't he try? . . . ." As if by the clearest effort of will, Ellen straightened in her chair and appeared to gain control of herself as she asked forcefully, "What was my mother's problem?"

Jacobs realized that he had made a mistake. If the Graysons had chosen to keep Martha's treatment a secret from the children, that was their decision, theirs alone. He had no right to tamper with their judgment. He simply had fallen into it before he realized what he was saying. At very least he must choose his words carefully and try to get on with his assessment of Ellen.

"She has been subject to low spirits, depressions, from time to time. We have worked together for many years, and there were times when she did not need my help, and we wouldn't meet for many months. My opinion, and I believe hers too, is that she has done very well. . . . I would suggest that you ask her about her experiences in treatment if you believe it would help you. Perhaps it would be best if you spoke directly with your mother." Jacobs allowed a short pause, then before Ellen could object he changed the subject and the tone of his voice. Straightening in his chair, he smoothed his hair back with his left hand as if to signal a return to the problem at hand.

"Well, now, let's get back to you. Fortunately, in recent years some very good medicine has been developed for treating depressions such as yours. And you need not feel that this would be an inferior form of treatment. Out here we believe in helping people feel better first. Then we try to take a look at the problems they face. It only seems right to take on problems when you feel up to it. How would you feel about a course of antidepressant medication?"

"Right now I simply want to get better. I'll give anything a try. But what if it doesn't work?" Ellen glanced up questioningly but was reassured by the expression on Jacob's face. He was not actually smiling, but his lips formed a tight, confident line and his face made a slight rhythmic, affirmative nodding motion.

"We will face that together if we have to. But I think it will work."

Tom did not want to be the first one to speak. He searched Ellen's face as she emerged from Marc Jacob's office, but found no clues. He hoped for some small sign, a smile perhaps, even some straightening of the humped shoulders that made her always appear so defeated. In fact, Ellen did move differently, Tom concluded, but the subtle change did not cheer him. Walking beside him, she fixed her gaze directly ahead as if pondering some matter that had been raised in Jacob's office. The burden of depression was still reflected in her face, but some new ingredient now complicated her expression. Ellen seemed enlivened, but in a distinctly negative sense. She was agitated rather than buoyant. Tom saw her hand trembling faintly as she grasped the door of the pickup. Something had happened with Jacobs, he realized. Maybe he should have asked to be included. Now he would just have to give Ellen a little time to settle.

After nearly 20 minutes of silence, Tom could remain calm no longer. He had managed to hold his tongue till then by becoming vaguely absorbed in the progress of an afternoon rainsquall that was setting up off to the northeast. He stole erratic, sidelong glances at the linear curtain of blues and grays until the edge of the slowly advancing weather crept into the periphery of his forward gaze. Then, maybe 15 miles off yet, he estimated. This is foolishness. Got to know what happened.

"Did Doc Jacobs have any good ideas, Ellie?"

Ellen did not respond. She appeared perplexed, almost dysphasic, as if the meaning of simple words had suddenly flown.

Tom persisted. "I don't want to pry into your business, now, but you are here with us, after all, and we can't help but worry."

Ellen recovered her voice, and managed to ask in a tone both fearful and resentful, "Why didn't you tell me that Mother had been a patient of Dr. Jacobs?"

Tom was taken by surprise. He had never really considered

Martha's treatment a secret. It was true that he and Martha had never discussed it with the children. Tom simply assumed that at some margin of awareness they, like he, knew their mother sometimes needed professional help. Ellen's question, in its accusatory tone, swept his habitual denial momentarily aside, and Tom heard himself respond defensively.

"Now I don't believe that's fair, Ellie, not fair at all. I . . . your mother and I . . . never lied to you."

"But you never told us either. Can't you understand what a shock this is to me?" Ellen protested bitterly.

"I guess I can . . . but no, maybe I can't, come to think of it. What difference does it make that your mother is a patient of Dr. Jacobs?"

"God, can't you see, Daddy? It means . . . I can't even start to think about everything it means . . . I'm almost afraid to . . . I've known Mother has her moods. Maybe this helps me understand some things . . . I think it does . . . but, now, all I can think of is that I've got the same problem, maybe it's in the family. . . . It seems so final."

"Look here, Ellie, I'm no doctor but I'm sure there's help. Things have changed plenty since Martha—your mother—had her trouble. What did Dr. Jacobs say?"

"He just gave me some medicine to take—but it all seems so futile now. If this thing is embedded in our family, I don't see how medicine can help. Probably nothing can."

Marc Jacobs had told Ellen that the medication would not work right away, maybe only after 2 or 3 weeks at the earliest. So when she woke on the fourth day after having started to take it, she was only vaguely aware that something was different. Actually, from the very first dose she had noticed that her mouth was continuously dry and that she was a bit lethargic. These side effects had all been explained to her. Now on that particular morning, referred to later as "the day things began to turn around," she became aware for the first time in years of the sun's gradual descent into the valley that rimmed the Grayson ranch. Often as a child she had wakened early on a gray-green mountain morning and watched with youthful anticipation for the first settling of sunlight atop the east-facing valley wall. There was something especially promising in this very visible contrast between darkness and light moving into one's world. Long before the sun had climbed above the eastern ridge, the perimeter of its warmth would advance slowly down the western boundary. As an adolescent on campouts, Ellen learned to stay in her bedroll until the "sun comes down" rather than up. On some occasions she and her fellow campers would decide to leave the comfort of body-warmed sleeping bags and at a signal run uphill to greet the sun. There they would be laughing, short of breath in the thin mountain air, darting over and around the pale green sage while a sagelike essence permeated the entire mountainside. For Ellen this memory was a prototype for joy. Almost every derivative experience, if pondered unhurriedly, led inevitably back to this, to the race for sunlight up a mountainside.

From there on, things moved rapidly. The very next day Ellen was dressed for breakfast and actually ate with the family. Since she had arrived in Trinidad, Ellen never left her room in the morning before 10 o'clock. Martha or Sarah would feed and entertain Little Tom in order that she might sleep late, but they were aware Ellen was usually awake long before dawn. Insomnia is debilitating enough, but combined with a pervasive lack of energy or interest, an inability to sleep becomes literal hell. Not only is one denied the usual physiological respite from care; in addition, the extra time awake is layered over with a pernicious disinterest in the common fare of consciousnes. So Ellen never slept late in the morning; she simply lay in bed and endured the slow progression of the day—insipid, colorless, moment after moment. Her appearance for breakfast, dressed and made up, moved David to glance quickly toward Sarah, then to his parents. Is it alright to say anything? he wondered. Ellen had quickly put an end to the family's nervous how-are-you's when she first arrived. David was not eager to hear again the dispirited, "Don't ask me that, please."

As usual, Tom could not help but make the observation aloud.

"You look mighty fine this morning, Ellie. . . . Feeling any . . . that is . . . sit down, here, right here, have some of Momma's famous eggs, you know how good—"

Martha interrupted Tom's nervous monologue, and he was relieved to have someone else take over the task of initiating conversation with Ellen. "You look a little brighter this morning, Ellen," she observed simply.

Almost as if accused, or at least suddenly encumbered with the obligation of being better in fact, Ellen sat down but did not reply for several moments, as if she were searching for a very carefully modulated disclaimer. For indeed she did note some improvement in her energy, in the morning, too; unusual, she realized. Still brief surges of liveliness had sometimes come upon her, even during the months when her depression seemed most unremitting. But they invariably came in the evening, often late, after Little Tom was in bed.

"I just decided to come down and have breakfast, that's all," she finally submitted, then added, "Do you mind?"

"Mind, why certainly not, dear. We're delighted, of course," Martha Grayson responded with the aplomb of a private-duty nurse. Tom found his vision suddenly blurred and realized in an instant the burden that his daughter's illness had become for him. Here he was, lunging at the vaguest hint of improvement, like a castaway at sea who had sighted a sprig of greenery floating past.

The next day it was even more obvious to Ellen and the family that her mood was changing. After sleeping soundly for 7 hours, she awoke refreshed, hungry, and anxious to help Martha with Little Tom's bath and breakfast. She talked of the trip to Alamosa, necessitated by an appointment with Jacobs, as if she were looking forward to the drive. The others were caught in a state of suspended amazement and hopeful thanksgiving. Sarah caught David's eye and winked. Tom found Martha looking at him with the expression of one who was observing a miracle in the offing, and shot a jaunty thumbs up back to her after Ellen had left the table. Surely, surely, the cloud was passing.

But Marc Jacobs was not altogether pleased. Indeed, the young woman who sat across from him in his consultation room was a very different Ellen. Gone was the set, woeful, look, the invariate lifelessness of the voice. Gone also the rounded shoulders, the stereotype of remorse typified by the clasping and unclasping of hands. Her greeting to him seemed genuine, even radiant. The mysterious animation of the face, pilgrim till now in regions unknown, had suddenly returned. Where there had previously been only a human form, now there was a woman, alive, responsive. Still Marc Jacobs worried.

It was simply too soon. The medication he had prescribed did not turn things around this rapidly, that is, not usually. And when it did, the process rarely plateaued out into a normal stable mood. He would have to adjust the dosage in an effort to abort a manic episode, he now realized, and while Ellen and the Graysons were sensing recovery, he must get them to understand that serious trouble could also be encountered at the opposite extreme. Only later, when he read Ellen's diary did Jacobs fully appreciate the nature of the change.

There is no way for me to communicate with anyone now so I must write, write to myself only. Write for myself. Also, because I have an urge to put my thoughts down for fear that I will forget them. And I must never forget. If I live to be ninety and become wise, fulfilled, and all the rest, I must never forget this time, this moment when I understood, when all of my doubts fell away and the universe opened up to me, like the solving of a great mystery. I can hardly remember the past year. It exists only as a dim spot in my memory, a small speck in the residue of a dream. I vaguely recall being depressed, hopeless, defeated by life. It is inconceivable to me now that I was ever that person, was ever hesitant, without hope nor any idea of a future. Now the future is broad, glorious, like a wide thoroughfare with every destination clearly marked.

I cannot understand this transformation. I do not want to understand it, if by understanding I will cause it to disappear. Here I am finally viewing my life, the people who love me, for the first time. I see everything in the clearest light. My father, my dear father, totally out of place in this family, but trying to do his best. I wish I could share these moments, these revelations, with him. We could cry together then, cry for all the times we have not been a family, for the times we have avoided each other, set our lives apart for fear of confrontation or argument or bad feeling. I'm not sure what would have come of it. Maybe nothing, maybe a great deal, maybe we would have discovered that we are not a family, that we are incapable of giving to each other, incapable of risking the truth. But then what is the truth in a family? If you cry over us, Daddy, does that mean you do not love us, that you do not love Mommy? Or has she been the source of our sorrow? Because we are sorrowful, you know. We are a weeping people, this household. No, you rarely see tears in our eyes, so do not look for them. We weep silently, we weep inwardly. Only our actions, never our faces, tell of the weeping. Watch us, watch our hands, the labored motions in one another's presence, these are the rituals of folks weeping, but only inwardly. If we wept outwardly, aloud, we would have to let one another see. And what then? Oh, god, what then?

Maybe she has been the source. Maybe Mother has kept us shy about our emotions. She is so unwilling to yield. I wish I had known her when she was young, even as a little girl. Did she become the way she is because her parents were cold, or weak, or maybe they were just parents and she, she herself cannot help it? Maybe she was born unaffectionate. I really don't believe that's possible but perhaps it is. Still she has set our tone. But can we blame her? What of Daddy, was he also at fault? How hard has he tried to open her up? I will never know the answer to that, I'm certain. There must have been times—when they were first married. God, how could they not have been forced to deal with each other out here. In the early years, during the long winters, the dusks at four o'clock and the dawns at eight. They must have talked to one another in those days. So I have to assume they have considered, debated, even fought about their relationship. There can be only one conclusion. She defeated him. What other possible truth is there? It is all around us, it has been ever since I can remember. They—he and she—never reached a decision. A truce, a gray, insipid, divided, lifeless, truce. God damn you! God damn you both—for cowardice, for weakness, for lack of courage. He has damned us after all, has he not? He has damned me through you, anyway. I am a loveless woman! I have everything that I could want. I appear whole, complete, there are no limbs missing, and I am even a little attractive. But

I am as hollow as a statue. What earthly good is a woman who cannot love? I do not know what my deficiency is. Is it genetic? Maybe it is! Maybe it is in our organs, swimming in our blood along with red blood cells and oxygen. Or maybe it is established in our tissues, deep in their automatic working, their chemistry. I can just see it there. An inability-to-love molecule, in every last cell, directing traffic, there forever, as much a part of me as every other molecule. In the dark, grey-blue hum of the cell's work it is there, unobtrusive, but making sure that its voice is always heard in the ultimate Ellen that lives, that moves about among people. If that's the case, I might as well forget it, forget even trying, simply accept this awful deficiency. Try to live with it. No, I never could—I would kill myself first. I could not consider living if I really believed there was no chance for me.

But now I know there is a chance. That is my great secret, God's own message to me, his inexpressible gift. In these last few weeks, even days, I have started to love again. It is as if a part of me that was dead had come alive. I feel love above me, around me, coursing through my veins. I am intoxicated with love. I feel recreated, born again, like the Baptist preachers say. Is this a religious conversion? Perhaps, I cannot say yet. I do feel a sense of security, a knowledge that I am protected, safe in the world, cared for, beloved. I have a tremendous sense of invulnerability, a knowledge—no, it's not knowledge—a direct apprehension of truth. A new direction. A wondrous, holy purpose.

I will put our houses in order. By my love I will give Mother and Daddy a new chance. I know I can explain to them the healing power that is available to everyone, the transcendent, reconciling power of love. Perhaps they are different. Maybe their goals and styles are like night and day. I know now that it doesn't matter. If they reach down inside themselves, reach out at the universe of love, to the source of life, they can find each other. Somewhere, beyond their differences, before and despite their differences, somewhere out there they are just Tom and Martha, my mother and father. They must get out that far, give themselves to the healing currents of rediscovery and rebirth.

They can do it, I know they can, with my help. I can sustain them when they get weary of trying, for my conviction will never waver. I can be a beacon to them, show them the way, even though I am only their daughter. I will be able to lead them, not as a little child, but as a woman, a woman who has somehow, by some great and gracious gift, come to see the answer to our separateness, to the division in our family, maybe even to the hostility among the nations of the world.

Then I will restore my marriage and my motherhood. I will look at my husband and he will know in an instant that the barriers are gone, that the underbrush has been thrust aside by the sharp, glittering blade of my new love. And I will turn to my son and he too will recognize, even in his infant understanding, that his mother has been restored to him. He will feel deep inside himself the rekindling of the universal fire of recognition—baby for mother. When I hold him he will know, beyond any rational process, that I am home, that he is mine, that we are a family once more. I will be able to sustain and support my husband in his work. Though he be tired and emptied of emotion, I will be able to restore his spirit from my reservoirs which are overflowing. He will only need to look into my eyes and he will be refreshed, filled again with my love which he can carry forth and distribute to those in need and yet retain in large measure for himself. We will know an intimacy which cannot be expressed. The depths of our togetherness will not be transmitted through the tools of spoken language or the written word. The fondest love poems will be like the weary testimonies of disillusioned lovers. Ours will be a love that flows between our souls like the dawn across a mountain, like electrons through space, a liquid force which travels with the speed of light.

I am certain that I can bring these things to pass. But what if I cannot? I shall not think of that. No, I shall, for what can I fear? If I have the gift of God, what can I fear? So I will think about every possibility, nothing will escape my careful analysis. If I cannot cause my parents to love each other, what then? They will go on as they have for years, honorably, separately, filled with loneliness, resentment, and the desolation of being apart. I could not accept it. No, I will never accept it. Perhaps my death would be the answer then. It is not unthinkable. In fact it occurs to me even as I am writing these very words that I must consider this possibility. In my thoughts just now I heard a distinct voice saying, "Yes, consider." So I will, I will! Oh. my god, maybe I have been on the wrong track! Maybe this story is destined to be a heroic tragedy. I never thought of it, but perhaps so. What makes me think this way? The clouds, perhaps, the day itself—cold, gray, raining. Is this a sign that no total happiness can come to pass without pain? Am I the necessary sacrifice for my family's happiness? I cannot bear to think this through any longer, I just cannot. But I must! If this is my lot, then so be it. It would be a high and worthy purpose for my life, that it be given for the reconciliation of my parents, for the liberation of my husband and child. If this is my role, then certainly I will be shown the way. I must be on the alert for signs that will come to me in unmistakable form. Oh, they may be disguised, they will have to be disguised, but I shall recognize them. They will be like clues broadcast among the common events of every moment. I will be able to read the messages imbedded in the matrix of the ebb and flow of the day. But I must be aware, I must be ready for meaning that is there, in nature, in the eyes of people who may be directing me as agents of a higher plan. God give me the eyes to see, the mind to read Thy will from the book of life.

I have just read over the first entries into my new journal, and I can only say that it is all coming to pass. Every detail of it seems to be working toward fulfillment and my life is central to it all. Today there were any number of signs. The first person I saw when I went for a walk this mornig was a neighbor who waved and held up two fingers, and I knew immediately that I had two choices. I could go forward, risk plumbing the depths of this revelation or retreat, go back to my previous state. He blew his horn three times and I am sure that meant the Trinity—Father, Son, Holy Ghost— all protecting me as I go through this challenging time in my life. I have no need for sleep. I lay awake nearly all night long and arose without any sense of fatigue—refreshed, ready to continue my pilgrimage. Mother and Daddy know too, I can tell. They will not say it openly, but I am sure they are aware of my new freedom, my release from the bondage of hopelessness and inaction. They are proud of me, I know that now. No matter what the future may bring, they will continue to be proud.

There it is again. I must consider! Should I sacrifice myself for the consummation of truth and intimacy in our family? Is this the way that I am being directed? Only time will tell. I must be watchful. There is so much meaning in the world, almost more than I can bear. How have I missed the messages before? They are all around me now. The whole world is conspiring to lead me in my new path. I feel special, chosen for a role that is more important, more demanding than any other. Can I hold up under this awful burden? I must, there is no other way.'

By the next night Tom Grayson knew something was terribly amiss with his daughter Ellen. Each day for about a week, since her depression had lifted, his doubts and fears had increased. He had watched her change first from a defeated, almost immobile creature into a wide-awake, enthusiastic woman, full of life and hope. His joy was without limits. "She is well, thanks be, she is well," he thought over and over. The next day, however, his happiness was colored with some concern. He noticed that she talked too much and never seemed to settle down. If she paused to sit for a moment in the midst of some rather wordy, abstract monologue, she soon rose to her feet again and paced back and forth as if rehearsing a part. For the first few days she finally fell asleep past midnight but was wide awake at 5 a.m. or so, setting the breakfast table and clattering about in the kitchen. That last night, however, neither Ellen nor Tom slept. Long after his wife Martha and the children had gone to bed, Tom remained downstairs fearing the worst. He and Martha had finally spoken about Ellen after dinner.

"What do you think is happening to her?" Martha finally broke the tense silence.

"I'm not sure, Martha, I'm just not sure. Something's not right, that's for certain."

"Do you think we should call Dr. Jacobs?"

"He must know something is wrong," Tom mused, almost to himself. "They met just 5 days ago, for God's sake."

"I know that. But she's gotten much worse since then. I can't get her to stop talking. And what's more, she's not making much sense. Everything is so glorious and meaningful, she says. She has one solution for her marriage, another for our family. I frankly can't stand to be around her. She starts attacking me for things she says I did when she was a child. Today she yelled at me, said that I had never been a mother to her. I can't take it anymore. One moment she's in some kind of bliss, the very next she is irritable and downright mean." Tom could sense the terror imbedded in Martha's complaining.

He finally prevailed, but Martha got him to agree to speak to Dr. Jacobs first thing the next morning, assuming that Ellen was no better. And there was no question that she was not better. In fact she was clearly worse. To begin with, Ellen refused to come out of her room when Tom, aware that she had slept little, if at all, knocked on her door soon after sunrise. He had dozed intermittently in his favorite lounging chair—a handsome, custom-built leather recliner to which he retired whenever he wanted to be alone. Interspersed with the brief awakenings, there had been fleeting dreams of Martha's hospitalization years before. He was watching her wake up from shock treatment, when she suddenly sprang from the recovery stetcher and tried to strangle him. He awoke with a rampant tachycardia and an ominous sense of inchoate dread, like a child emerging from a nightmare. The whole night had been like that. The terror he sought to flee in the blessed interludes of sleep stalked him relentlessly on the other side of consciousness. So he had been finally relieved to see the dawn, to have an excuse to go up to Ellen's room.

At first there was no answer to his knocking, although he could hear her moving about inside the room. Then Ellen answered; that is, Tom knew it could only be Ellen, but he scarcely recognized her voice.

"No, you can't come in. No one is allowed inside. There is no role for you in this. The future is clear."

"Ellie . . . dear . . . it's me, your father, Tom. . . ."

"No, you're not my father. You may look like my father but you are not. . . . You are an imposter sent here to torment me."

"Now, Ellie, don't be ridiculous. Let me in; let me talk to you."

"Don't you dare try to come into this room!" The voice was wild, imperative, and frightening. "If you try to come in I'll . . . I'll destroy myself. I can destroy us all with my mind and I will not hesitate to do it. . . ."

Tom felt himself on the brink of total panic. He wanted to break down the door, not so much to get to Ellen as to strike out against the awful anxiety that had beset him. He tried to control himself, and with clumsy, backward steps moved down the stairs. He groped for the telephone in the early morning light.

Jacobs' phone must have rung 15 times before there was an answer. It was still very early, Tom suddenly realized.

"Hello . . . Dr. Jacobs," the voice was muffled and sleepy on the other end.

"Dr. Jacobs . . . Tom Grayson here. Doc, there is something awful wrong with Ellen. She's like a wild woman, talking crazy and saying I'm not her father. . . . Oh my God, Doc, she must be going out of her mind . . . I just don't know what to do. . . ."

"Now, Mr. Grayson, try to calm yourself. What exactly has happened?"

"Doc, I just don't know. She seemed to be getting better, you know, for a while anyway. Then she got sorta excited, talked too much, seemed so irritable and all in the last few days. Then yesterday it all got worse. She hadn't slept for a couple of nights . . . and now, Jesus, Doc, she's just . . . well, completely gone, out of her mind. . . ."

"I was afraid of that," came the faint reply.

"What did you say, Doc? Tom shot back.

"I just meant to say that I had been worried that Ellen might be getting pretty high. It sounds like she's developed a manic attack. That sometimes occurs following a severe depression. . . . she may have to be hospitalized, Mr. Grayson."

"Oh, Jesus. . . . Well, where . . . I mean how can we do that? She won't even open her door."

"I'll get on the phone right away, to see if I can get a bed—"

"Doc, what should I do here—I just don't know how to handle her."

"Try to be calm. Don't force her. Just assure her that help will be on the way, that I am coming, and that we are going to see that she gets proper medical attention."

"Okay, Doc, I'll try. We'll do our best, but, please . . . please hurry. . . . Doc, will she get over this? Can this kind of thing get better?"

"Yes, certainly, Mr. Grayson, but she will need rest and some medication."

"Okay . . . all right, at least I know something can be done. . . . hurry, Doc, try to get here real soon."

"I'll have to make a few calls and I'll be on my way."

Jacobs' car roared up the lane to the Grayson's house just as the sun rose above the eastern ridge of foothills that cradled the Grayson property. Both driver and car were enveloped in a cloud of dust when finally Jacobs emerged carrying a small black medical bag.

"Where is she?" Jacobs asked, without any other greeting, wiping the dirt from his eyes.

"She's still upstairs in her room, Doc. . . . I can't get her to come out," Tom replied dejectedly. The lack of sleep coupled with the unstinting pressure of a nameless dread for his daughter's safety, had begun to wither his spirit. Moving almost automatically, he followed Jacobs into the house. Out of the corner of his eye, Jacobs saw Martha Grayson huddled in one corner of a leather sofa, her face in her hands, as if she were trying to will away this moment of her life.

For a few minutes Jacobs tried to coax Ellen to unlock the door, but there was no answer to his firm but gentle entreaties. For just an instant he paused and rubbed his face, as if thinking, or perhaps marking an end to ceremonies of civility. Looking up resolutely, he turned to Tom, who had stopped two steps shy of the second floor landing and who now stood with head bowed, supporting himself by gripping the heavy oak bannister with both hands.

"We'll have to break down the door," Jacobs said sadly.

"You what? . . . Of course, Doc, whatever you say," Tom muttered, almost unbelievingly.

Jacobs backed away about a step and suddenly kicked the door just beside the pearl-white handle with a ferocity that seemed to startle Tom back to his senses. They both rushed in as the door swung open and the shattered latch mechanism made a sound like a pistol shot against the opposite wall.

Ellen lay coiled in the corner clothed only in a soiled night-gown. Tom later recalled that he hardly recognized her at that moment. Her hair completely obscured her face except for her dark eyes that peered out as if from a forest thicket. The soles of her feet were black with dirt, and the room was rank with the odor of perspiration. He thought, she is a wild fawn, way off somewhere in the meadow, thinking we are going to destroy her. But we won't hurt you, little thing . . . we want to save you . . . please don't be afraid . . . please, baby, it's just me and Doc Jacobs.

So primitive was Ellen's expression that neither man at first dared to touch her. Jacobs, swallowing hard, realizing that his throat was leathery with fear, spoke first. "Now, Ellen, everything is going to be all right. . . . You hear, do you hear me, Ellen?" There was no reply. The wild eyes did not blink. "Now, Ellen, I'm going to give you an injection that will let you sleep. . . . You have been very upset and need to sleep. . . ."

Jacobs fumbled with his bag at first but finally opened it. He quickly withdrew a syringe and a vial of sodium amytal. Snapping the end of the vial, he adroitly drew up the liquid while watching Ellen intently.

"Hold this," he commanded Tom, as he dug back into his bag and produced a small rubber tourniquet and an alcohol sponge. He approached Ellen cautiously and took her right arm, which was thrown carelessly across her thighs. Ellen appeared not to notice as he slipped the tourniquet under her arm and tightened it just above the elbow. Then she began to sob, quietly but with a resignation that was at once a relief and a desolation to her audience.

"Kill me, kill me, please kill me," she pleaded, as if invoking one final, coveted option that alone had kept her alive. Jacobs found the vein on the first attempt, pulled back a wisp of dark red blood, and slowly began to press the plunger of the syringe into the barrel. There was no protest. Ellen's animal-like stare began to soften, her lids fell and rose again several times before closing and remaining shut. Her whole body seemed to embrace the oblivion that now pervaded its most distal cellular recesses. She urinated a foul-smelling liquid. Tom stepped forward when

Jacobs had withdrawn the syringe and gathered Ellen up like a newborn calf. He could scarcely see through his tears as he carried her down the stairs.

Marc Jacobs had not told Tom and Martha Grayson that there were no beds available at the University Hospital in Denver. The admitting physician had suggested they take Ellen to the state hospital until a bed became available. Jacobs had argued forcefully, but to no avail. He then decided to wait until they were well on their way to inform the Graysons of the problem, and was relieved when Tom urged Martha to remain at home. Jacobs sensed Martha's precarious state of mind and was not anxious to have to explain the boarding arrangement he had been forced to accept. It would be difficult enough telling Tom. No need to explain right away, he thought. Tom rode in the back seat with Ellen's sleeping form alongside; her head rested on a pillow in his lap. He held her gingerly and from time to time smoothed her hair as if to make sure that beneath the snarled and unkept strands lay his daughter's face. Ellen breathed with the slow, regular rhythm of an anesthetized person; as she inhaled, her entire body seemed to inspire, and miniature bubbles formed on her swollen lips as air escaped. The regularity of her breathing was comforting to Tom. At least something about her appeared intact, regular, dependable. He thought, How can this be Ellen? What in God's name has happened? God help her. . . . God help us all.

They drove for nearly half an hour in a strained silence, which Tom finally interrupted.

"About an hour to the hospital, you figure, Doc?"

"Well . . . actually, Mr. Grayson, we won't be going that way today," Jacobs replied apologetically.

"We what? How do you mean?"

"I couldn't get a bed. . . . they are full up. Ellen will have to be boarded for a little while at the state hospital—just a few days, I'm sure." "Goddam, Doc. Why can't those bastards . . . I mean, one lousy bed. Stop at the next gas station, Doc, I'll get on the phone . . . I know some people . . . I'll get a bed."

"I wouldn't advise it, Mr. Grayson. If they say they're full, we have to accept it. . . . I'm sure something will open up soon, and in the meantime she can get started on medication and—"

"No, sir . . . not the state hospital. I know about those places. No daughter of mine is going to be in a nuthouse full of God knows what kind of people. . . . No, can't have it, Doc. Please stop and let me call soon as you can."

Resignedly, Jacobs murmured "Okay, have it your way."

A Mobil sign appeared in the distance near the apparent vertex of the parallel fence rows bordering the highway. As Jacobs pulled in for gas, Tom gently lifted Ellen's sleeping head from his lap, jumped from the car, and jogged toward a public phone booth standing nearby. The floor and walls of the cubicle were spotted with a dried residue deposited by nameless tobacco chewers; countless phone numbers were etched into fading, pale-green paint.

Jacobs waited nearly half an hour and watched Tom dial perhaps a dozen numbers—imploring, gesturing more violently each time with his free hand. Finally he saw Tom slap the side of the booth with a closed fist, so forcefully that the entire flimsy structure tipped percariously. The startled station attendant strolled over, an older man with bronzed skin, not easily excited.

"Easy there, friend. If you lost a dime, just let me know."

"Goddam fucking doctors. . . . When you really need 'em they treat you like shit. . . . I'm gonna get my senator on this . . . you just wait." Tom was mumbling to himself.

"Anything I can help you with?" the attendant tried again.

"No . . . hell, no . . . seems like there's no help anywhere for the Graysons," Tom replied defeatedly as he slumped back into Jacobs' car.

The state hospital had been built at the turn of the century on a prominent hill north and east of the city. Constructed as a showpiece of humane care for the mentally ill, it was originally a self-contained economic unit. Cows were milked and butter was processed; fields of corn and melons produced bountifully with the critical nurturance of a well-maintained irrigation system dug by hand and shovel from the flanks of the river. In those early days, patients were put quickly to work in the fields or along the ditches; there was always room for one more hoe or shovel. And the work seemed to be therapeutic in itself, so long as the crews avoided the heat of July and August and the bitter cold of midwinter. Originally some ten buildings housed approximately 5,000 patients; 3,000 would never leave, 2,000 would leave at least once, sometimes for good.

Then in the 1940s, a variety of well-intentioned individuals began to become troubled about this and similar institutions throughout the country. Concerns over "institutional peonage" were raised, and legislation was ultimately passed making it illegal to put a psychiatric patient to work in a state institution. Daytime ward censuses rose dramatically, and violence among patients as well as regressive apathy increased. With the advent of the psychopharmacologic era and more active rehabilitation programs, 5 out of the original 10 buildings were closed, and the hospital population dropped below 2,000. There arose a new catchword—*deinstitutionalization*—a concept that, for all its legitimate optimism, implied that the state hospitals, once created to fashion hope out of shattered lives, had themselves become the problem and not part of the solution. State mental health directors were required to use part of the money budgeted for hospitals to support fledgling, inadequately conceived community care facilities, because few states were willing to provide the additional funds implied by the concept of community-based care. The crusaders either did not understand the nature of clinical reality in severe mental disorder or they grossly overestimated societal commitment to the legacy of Dorothea Dix. State mental health resources were spread too thin, and a serious decline in service was inevitable. Unless one had no other options, one did not send a family member or a patient to a state hospital. Marc Jacobs knew this was indeed the case, but he was certain Ellen would be there a few days only.

The admission unit at first did not create such a negative impression. The newest of the hospital buildings, it had been able to avoid the harsh geometric perfection of the earlier structures. Its low, two-story lines, and rather rambling design formed a visually manageable pattern. It was basically a brick structure, air-conditioned, with shock-proof glass in the second-floor windows. The grass was sloppily mowed but not raked, and two small flower beds near the entrance were untrimmed and unkept, although several clutches of marigolds and various voluntary wild flowers maintained a dash of color.

Moving about the grounds singly and in random patterns

were those almost indescribable figures, the long-term residents of such institutions who, entrusted with complete freedom of the place, seemed to roam at will like pet deer. The hospital would be their final home, for they were without meaningful connection to the outside world. Inwardly they were spent, exhausted—"burned out" was the phrase that newly hired aides found descriptive and used all too hastily. Invariably they looked odd, even before one could make out the blank faces and the busy lips, which sometimes gave forth audible sounds and sometimes did not. Their strangeness was apparent in their form, their posture. Arms appeared too lengthy for bodies, heads seemed almost to disappear between stooped shoulders. Such individuals attended only to the ground, and never made eye contact with the workers who came and went, shift after shift. These ground wanderers acted as if they were invisible and were similarly regarded.

Marc Jacobs did not use the front entrance, however. Because Ellen was still asleep from the amytal, he turned down a one-lane road leading to the rear of the building and parked near a stenciled red sign that designated "Emergency Admissions."

Jacobs asked Tom to wait in the car with Ellen while he made preliminary arrangements for admission. Through the window Tom could see Jacobs pacing back and forth in a dimly lit room. He was chain-smoking and Tom thought, even guys who've been through this get nervous. I'm not the only one strung clean out, I reckon. Damn nice of Doc Jacobs to drive us all this way. . . . I'm gonna see you through it, baby. Don't know what all this means but I'm gonna be right there with you. Tom at last saw Jacobs stride across the floor resolutely with his hand extended. A smiling figure of darker complexion met him at the midpoint of the room. Then both men disappeared from the view Tom had. Sitting down now and going over her story, I guess, Tom theorized to himself. After about 20 minutes he was startled by a tap on his shoulder. He had dozed off briefly and was suddenly surprised to see Jacobs' face at the open window; Tom inhaled the stale, pungent air that attends chain smokers and felt a wave of nausea.

"The doctor wants to talk to you for a few minutes. . . . Dr.

Pablo Leon . . . seems like a decent enough guy. I'll stay with Ellen until they're ready to take her up."

Without answering, Tom opened the door, thankful to be able to move about and breathe freely. The nausea seemed to diminish long enough for him to climb the three wooden steps and enter the office where Dr. Leon was waiting, seated behind a bare desk, the color of file-cabinet green.

"Good afternoon, Mr. Grayson," Dr. Leon spoke with a very slight accent as he rose, "I am Dr. Pablo Leon, the admitting psychiatrist today."

Pablo Leon was a gentle-looking man of about 30, less than average height, with a businesslike appearance. His face was swarthy but without lines, and his silver-rimmed glasses gave him the appearance of a diffident English teacher. His eyes were dark but friendly and conveyed an expression of chronic fatigue, not quite resignation. He wore a full-length white coat, in need of both laundering and pressing. The bulbous head of a reflex hammer slouched outside of a large side pocket on the right. The companion pocket on the left was completely packed with a small black notebook and an assortment of dog-eared pieces of paper, including several large-sized envelopes. One got the impression that he had not found the time to open his mail in several days.

"Glad to meet you, Dr. Leon . . . Tom Grayson . . . my daughter Ellen's the patient. . . ."

"So I understand. I wonder if I could ask you a few questions before we take her up the the ward?"

"Sure . . . Okay. You understand, Dr. Leon, that Ellen will be going to the University Hospital just as soon as I . . . as we . . . can get her in there. . . ."

"Dr. Jacobs told me that you would like to have her admitted in town as soon as possible."

"Yes, that's right. . . . No offense, you understand, Doc. It's just that . . . well . . . her mother was once . . . oh, hell it's a long story . . . say we want her there for personal reasons."

"I think I understand, Mr. Grayson. Now just let me get a little information from you."

It seemed to Tom that the questions were predictable: full name; age; the date and circumstances of her delivery; when she first walked, talked; how she did in the first grade. After 15 minutes or so, when Dr. Leon had just asked whether Ellen had smoked marijuana as a teenager, Tom felt his patience ebbing.

"Doc, I tell you, could you and I finish this after we get Ellie settled. She's asleep just now and needs—"

As Tom was finishing his sentence, Marc Jacobs rushed into the room looking panicky.

"Tom, Dr. Leon, come help me with Ellen! She's waking up and I can't handle her." Tom rushed outside with Dr. Leon in his white coat following closely.

Ellen was standing unsteadily behind the opened rear door of Jacob's car in her underwear.

"Help me get these things off . . . I'm suffocating . . . clothes are not important now . . . don't touch me!" A scream ensued that pierced Tom like a dull knife. Jacobs reached into the car and threw a blanket around Ellen, which she discarded with a wild sweep of both arms. Instinctively, Tom picked her up, then stood dazed and immobile while her arms and legs made aimless, flailing motions.

"Bring her into the office!" Dr. Leon shouted, trying simultaneously to control Ellen's legs. His glasses caught the brunt of a random kick and were propelled somewhere into the afternoon. Tom and Jacobs managed somehow to get Ellen's writhing form back into the admitting office, and Dr. Leon, without glasses, motioned toward a stretcher in the corner of the room. In the meantime, two aides, an obese, blond woman and a black youth, had arrived and skillfully managed to get canvas restraints secured to Ellen's four thrashing limbs. Even in the restraints, her torso gyrated like a woman in painful labor, and her shrieks of protest contributed to the image of childbirth in some primitive setting.

Dr. Leon picked up the phone and dialed three digits. "Mrs. Tompkins, bring 50 of Thorazine to emergency, right away. Thank you."

After an hour or so of helpless struggling, plus two 50-milligram injections of Thorazine deep in her buttocks, Ellen fell asleep again. It was not the ponderous amytal sleep, however, because she could be wakened with gentle shaking and a strongly-spoken inquiry.

"Ellen, this is Dr. Leon speaking. Can you hear me? We are going to take you up to the ward now. You will be all right there. We will see to it that you get plenty of rest and medication. Do you want to say anything to your father and Dr. Jacobs first?"

"You mean I can't go up with her?" Tom blurted out. "Please, Doc, I won't be in the way."

"I'm sorry, Mr. Grayson. You can come back at 7 o'clock, during visiting hours."

Tom did not reply, simply dropped both hands to his side, and bowed his head in an ultimate gesture of resignation. He walked slowly over to the stretcher where Ellen lay and took her hand in both of his while he spoke in a whisper.

"I gotta leave you now, Ellie . . . but I'll be back soon. The doctors are going to help you as long as you're here . . . and as soon as we can we're taking you to town. . . . God bless you, baby."

"C'mon with me, Tom," Jacobs interrupted. "Let me buy you some supper." The two men turned and left the admissions office. Tom's movements reflected his ultimate weariness. Jacobs was at his side, gently supporting him with an arm.

When Ellen awoke she did not know where she was. The charge nurse, Sophie Tompkins, noticed Ellen's stirring just after she came on duty and was at her bedside when the light of day finally broke through Ellen's confused consciousness. The drug had already begun to subdue the conflagration that had consumed her thinking for at least a week, like a gentle rain descending upon a timber fire that had long been burning beyond control.

Sophie Tompkins was a very good psychiatric nurse. She had been in charge on the acute unit for 15 years and ran the ward with benevolent firmness. She had seen nearly everything during her career, and somehow managed to maintain an optimistic, disciplined love for her work. A widow for 10 years, she lived with her mother and a 20-year-old mongoloid son, and on her days off she took her son hiking in the mountains. The sturdiness of her figure was mirrored in her movements. Seemingly in endless motion throughout the day, she managed to have a brief conversation with each of her 50 or so patients in between medication rounds, doctors' visits, and ward meetings. Her physical strength was a legend at the hospital. She once personally restrained a 200-pound male who in a paranoid rage had attacked one of her aides, yet she tolerated no wanton violence on the part of her staff. If a staff member struck a patient, he was summarily escorted off the ward by Sophie and rarely returned to work there. The hospital superintendent, Manley Hughes, trusted Sophie's clinical and administrative judgment completely. He knew she was one of those rare individuals capable of remaining in an acute-psychiatric setting without becoming embittered, hardened, and sadistic. Only once had he intervened and asked her to take a month away from the hospital. That suggestion occurred following two consecutive suicides on the unit; Sophie seemed to take the deaths very personally, and finally asked Hughes to reassign her to another ward. Instead he gave her a month with pay, and Sophie went to Europe with her son, where she visited psychiatric hospitals in several countries. On her return she had regained her spirit and began to put into practice some of the methods she had seen during her trip.

"Ellen, I am Sophie Tompkins, the charge nurse on 2 West here. You have been quite out of sorts for over a week, Dr. Jacobs tells me. We are going to try to begin treatment here. Then as soon as there is a bed in town, you will be transferred there. How are you feeling?"

"Not so good, very weak, tired," Ellen replied. Then the chaos began to return, the clouds closed over, and her fragile composure started to slip away.

"I feel very frightened. Something is going to happen, something important. I know it. I believe I am part of a new consciousness, I have a special role . . . but I am so afraid. . . . What was that?" (A door slammed somewhere on the ward.) "Who are all these people? Do they know who I am?

"There is nothing to be frightened about. These folks are all other patients. You are extra sensitive now, to yourself, to sounds, to people, everything. That's part of your illness. What's important is rest—rest and routine. When you feel your thoughts crowding in on you, let me know. Then we'll talk more. You can be alone whenever you wish."

Ellen did not reply at first. This woman seemed pleasant, but she obviously did not understand, or else . . . perhaps she knew but was playing dumb. It was best to go along with her for now.

"I'll be alright. Thanks."

"I'll be around if you need me."

Recovering from psychosis is a slow and uneven process. When periods of clarity first begin to appear, they can be almost as bewildering as the beginning of the illness itself. When one is delusional, at least there is meaning, even if it is idiosyncratic meaning. There can be strange comfort in a delusional world, particularly when the world of reality brings only reminders of life at an impasse. As this state of mind loses complete dominion, new questions arise. For several days during early recovery, consciousness is a literal battlefield that endures in waves the surges of unreason and the first counterattacks of consensus reality. During this fragile period, patients are extremely vulnerable to individuals who, out of ignorance or cynical self-interest, are in a position to exploit them.

Ellen prepared for bed and for her second night in the hospital. During the day she had managed to contain her delusional ideas for the most part. Twice she had spoken with Sophie Tompkins, and twice she had elected to spend a "quiet period" in a room by herself. Away from the stimulation of the unit, her seething consciousness seemed to relent gradually. She had received her medication three times during the day, her final dose only a few minutes before she was ready to try to sleep.

Ward 2 at the state hospital was made up of two units, a 25-bed female unit and a male unit of identical size. The two sections were separated by a hallway and by the locked doors of the units themselves. Both male and female sides were composed of an open section that contained 19 beds in a single large room, plus three 2-bed units nearest the nursing station where newly admitted patients were first assigned. Ellen was placed in one of the 2-bed rooms; the other bed was unoccupied. The lavatory was just off the nursing station near her room. As she left her room to wash up, she noticed a light in the nursing station, but realized that it was unoccupied. A tall man, about 30, wearing white trousers and a white tee shirt, entered the ward.

Ellen, dressed in a long flannel nightgown, approached him and asked, "Is there a nurse on duty here? I'd like to use the lavatory."

"I'm Stuart Adams, the aide covering both sides. I can let you in."

Somewhat embarrassed, Ellen replied, "Oh, all right, thank you . . . you know you look like someone I know."

Adams, taken a bit by surprise, replied, "Is that so? I haven't seen you here before."

"No, I was just admitted today."

Stuart Adams had been unemployed until the previous week. A year before he had been laid off from a construction job, and when his unemployment income was about to end, he applied for work at the hospital. Such hospitals always have aide positions open. The pay is meager and the turnover is high, so the employment office does not ask any questions. The man who hired Adams failed to find out that he had a substantial police record and had done a year's time for armed assault. His first and only marriage had ended 3 years before; his wife charged him with repeated brutality during their 4 years together. That he had been a camp counselor for 2 years as a teenager had apparently meant something to the employment people. They did not know that he had been fired for molesting female campers. Adams had been hired on the spot, for the hospital needed large male aides. In-service training would teach him what he needed to know, and was scheduled to begin the following week. In the meantime, "Just try to stay awake and break up fights," the interviewer had said jokingly as he shook Adams' hand.

Severe impulsivity may be the personal attribute most incompatible with mental health work. Fortunately, individuals with moderate problems in this area are not usually attracted to mental health disciplines. Occasionally they are, however, and it becomes the responsibility of training programs to weed out the recalcitrant ones before they use patients badly. Of course, such safeguards are irrelevant in many state institutions, where the majority of the caretakers have had no serious preparation for their work whatsoever. They, like Stu Adams, simply put in their time and treat patients the way they treat other people in their lives who excite, frustrate, or oppose them.

Ellen turned when she heard the door of the lavatory open again, expecting to see another patient. Instead, Adams stood in the dimly lit room staring at her.

"What are you doing in here?" she demanded.

"I came to check on you. No reason to be frightened."

"Please leave, please leave me alone," Ellen's plea sounded more like a supplication than a demand.

Adams walked toward her, speaking softly, "Now don't you be afraid. You're gonna like me. I'm gonna make you feel real good."

"Oh God!" Ellen protested, retreating against a wall. She tried to scream, but her mouth was so dry that the cry surged forth in muffled staccato.

It may have been a blessing that her illness was still available to her, for she fled to the refuge of its exalted promises where all pain was transmuted into purpose. She was no longer there, but away somewhere in gray-blue space. She scarcely felt the towel around her face, the push, the impact of the white-tiled floor, and the final violations of the body she had abandoned in her flight.

Immediately and instinctively, Sophie realized that something dreadful had happened to Ellen during the night; from sad experience she suspected the truth. Ellen was found by the first arrivals on the morning shift, lying outside the unlocked lavatory; she was awake but virtually catatonic with some bruises about the face. Sophie dialed the superintendent's office and spoke with her eyes closed.

"Manley, this is Sophie. . . . Manley, it's happened here again. . . . Yes, I'm afraid so . . . not a nobody this time either. . . . Yes, the Grayson woman, was supposed to be transferred. . . . Manley, will you let me deal with it my way? . . . No publicity, I promise you. . . . All right, all right, let's say I never asked you. . . . We can do it that way, too. . . . Thanks, Manley."

That evening when Stuart Adams reported for work, Sophie was on hand to greet him, accompanied by five very large but very trusted male aides. Her aides had bet Sophie that Adams would not show up. From the window of 2 West, the female patients could see an unusual cluster of seven people walking toward Robman 2, a long-deserted building near the rear of the hospital grounds. Two uniformed hospital employees had linked arms with a man wearing a denim suit; three other men also in uniform surrounded the trio. A sturdy woman in white brought up the rear. It was indeed a strange procession. Suggesting at first a gathering of friends out for an evening stroll, the group had a more precise destination in mind.

When they finally emerged from Robman 2 thirty minutes later, these same individuals approximated their previous formation, with one obvious difference, however. The one man not in uniform was being supported totally now by the aides; his head hung limply forward and bounced rhythmically as his two supporters literally swung his legs forward with each step, using their underarm grips as a fulcrum. Occasionally Adams raised his head as if to protest and made the soundless mouth opening movements of a fish on dry land. When the group passed beneath the overhead light marking the walkway, one could make out the bloodied matting of hair that covered his face like dried paint. Before the aides had delivered Sophie's remedy, she had fired Stuart Adams and had warned him that the hospital would have him arrested if he were recognized on the grounds ever again. To anyone's knowledge, he never tested her resolve.

The following morning, after speaking again with Manley Hughes, Sophie had immediately phoned Sara Saulsbury, Director of Nursing at Colorado Psychopathic and her lifelong friend. Sophie and Sara essentially managed patient traffic between the two institutions. In so doing, they kept their respective superintendents notified but not necessarily informed. Within an hour Ellen had been sedated and was dozing in a hospital car on her way to Denver in the company of two female aides as well as Sophie, who had simply reported to Jacobs that a bed had unexpectedly become available. Word was left at the motel where Tom was staying, informing him of the immediate transfer and citing "state regulations" as forbidding the movement of patients by private vehicle. He would be able to meet his daughter in Denver by early afternoon, the note stated. Sophie was counting on Tom's thankfulness for the transfer overcoming any annoyance with its abruptness, and she calculated correctly.

"I'll be goddam . . . if that don't beat anything I ever saw," he murmured as he stared at the note while standing in the lobby of the motel.

Ellen continued treatment with another psychiatrist in Denver, Dr. Saul Enroe, following her hospitalization. Not that she disapproved of Marc Jacobs; in fact she later realized that his involvement in her hospitalization had at least been well intended and very possibly lifesaving. Her willingness to be followed by someone else was born out of a growing awareness that she and

Jacobs would never be able to work past the issue of his role in her hospitalization.

For Ellen, the actual events of the state hospital remained forever just beyond the reach of accurate recall. Yet in her dreaming, which she later often described to Saul Enroe, the episode became an unconscious repository for fantasies of denigration and helplessness.

"There was this man, an attendant I think, on the unit . . . and then . . . all I remember is fear . . . awful fear . . . maybe he hurt me . . . or maybe I fainted from the medication. . . ." Even though Ellen's associations to her most frightening dreams never led much further, Enroe guessed what might have happened. He debated whether to share his suspicions with her, but decided not to force the issue. Perhaps it will emerge in time, he thought. Neither of them considered the possibility of attempting to find out by actually going back to the hospital and questioning Sophie Tompkins or other members of the staff. Enroe received a hospital summary a month after Ellen arrived in Denver, which read in part:

> The second night after admission the patient slept poorly and was still very psychotic. Nursing staff reported that she was up and wandering about the ward much of the time. The following morning she was found to be even more disorganized and showed evidence of a fall sometime during the night. She then received chlorpromazine 200 mg p.o. and was transferred to Denver by hospital motor pool.

So much for the complicity of hospital records, he thought. We'd have to ask for an investigation, and even then I'm not sure it would help Ellen. Perhaps better to put it all behind us and go on from here.

RETROSPECTIVE

The third chapter of this book is devoted to the stories of individuals whom I knew for an extended period of time. The experience of following patients over several years is critical for the maturation of the psychiatric clinician. I am not necessarily referring to intensive contact, but rather simply to the opportunity to be in touch with an individual long enough to get to know him in his own milieu and oneself as reflected by that process. As a rule, the more prolonged the relationship with a patient is, the more that person sheds the status of patienthood and comes to be regarded as a fellow human being.

In the case of Elaine, we were never able to achieve an alliance that was sufficiently strong to sustain the treatment. Perhaps my inexperience was to blame. As the story indicates, I was vulnerable to her challenges of my competence and sensitivity. Working with her over time, I came to appreciate the myriad faces of her disorder and the temptation to react either to her praise and adulation or to her contempt. And her suicide again called forth all the darkness and self-doubt that I had experienced following the death of Captain Wilson. There were no excuses this time. She had been my patient in every way, and I had worked conscientiously with her for over a year under regular and careful supervision. It may have been Freulich's response to her suicide that salvaged my self-esteem, for he seemed to have been as affected as I was. The day that I told him, he asked to be excused for a few moments and left my office. When he returned 15 minutes or so later, it was obvious to me that his eyes were red. He simply stated that he hated to see life slip away so needlessly. Our supervisory relationship changed after Elaine's suicide. We became much closer than before, and I sensed that he regarded me as a colleague as well as a student.

My relationship with Miles extended over many years. We were like travelers on a journey together, the extent of which neither of us fully appreciated at the beginning. When we first began working together, I was relatively inexperienced, so that in a very real way I grew in the relationship as well as he. Early on in the therapy I had hoped that Miles' improvement would come about at a faster pace. Once we had gained control of his major symptoms I rather assumed that his development would continue unimpeded. But it did not happen that way. Despite the absence of incapacitating symptoms, Miles still had subtle but critical difficulties in two important areas—intimate relationships and work. With regard to relationships, he experienced great difficulty negotiating the small, almost automatic sequences that this process demands. In groups he was painfully self-conscious; this crippling preoccupation with the ways others were perceiving and evaluating him led to his avoiding small, informal social gatherings altogether. His handicap proved to be exceptionally resistant to modification and seriously impaired his capacity to work as well as to cultivate friendships. In the work setting he was overly sensitive to critical comments, his ear always tuned to this expectation. When he would meet a woman he liked, he would become obsessed with her and had trouble following the guidelines of reasonable reciprocity in his quest for a special relationship. With all his problems in these areas, however, he helped me appreciate the complexity of mature capacities in these two fundamental domains. How intricate and demanding is the making of a friend and the completion of a task! As I began to see the magnitude of the developmental challenges Miles was facing, I also began to have another view of our work together. I felt more comfortable being myself, offering constructive suggestions, telephoning an employer when it seemed important to do so. I was able to see improvements, but the process was substantially slower than I had expected. Miles taught me what I had been trying to teach him—the importance of patience and of persistence; above all, persistence.

The story about Carol illustrates another important lesson that becomes apparent with time. In the process of learning another life story well, one begins to care about that life. Indeed, unless there is a strong positive regard between psychiatrist and patient, chances are that the treatment will not be very successful. However, there are complexities here as well that cannot be overlooked; this work has the capacity to create and promote self-deception in the mind of the therapist. Working at this close confessional distance, one may come to think of oneself as the therapeutic agent rather than as the facilitator of a therapeutic process. Or, as in the story, one may become vulnerable to particular transference behaviors because of the stage and circumstances of one's own life. In psychiatric work, as in living, it is good to have one's personal needs under reasonable control.

The story of Randy is intended to underscore another process that depends essentially upon time: namely, a sense of history. Randy himself trained during another period of intense ferment in the field. Psychological theories had found fertile ground in America, and psychological treatment methods as primary therapies were being applied beyond the confines suggested even by Freud himself. On the other hand, the first significant somatic treatments were being pioneered in Europe. Even though he had been tutored by some famous men, Randy himself did not become famous in the same sense. To those who knew him, however, he was someone who honored his profession by the way he conducted himself with his patients. He was doggedly devoted to helping them. It was primarily his commitment, not his method, that one remembers. And he made it clear that such professional tenacity was not native in him, but was kindled and sustained by his teachers.

Ellen is a personal tale whose central elements I know very well. If one stays in the field of psychiatry over an extended period, eventually patienthood will find you. Whether in the context of one's own personal therapy or on the occasion of difficulty in the life of someone close, it is inevitable, and perhaps even just, that one will experience the profession from the other side. Such experiences, to my mind, are more vivid and startling than one usually imagines ahead of time. It is not simply that the meaning of psychological pain comes home in a wholly unique and unforgetable manner. That happens. However, one also learns how significant our therapies can be for the individual sufferer, assuming of course that one gets into the hands of someone capable. Being a patient or knowing one as close as family is an experience, in my estimation, roughly equivalent to all the didactic instruction one receives in terms of its relevance for an ultimate sense of profession in psychiatry.

I have therefore written about these lives in an effort to present the span of adult psychiatry as I have come to know it. My purpose has been to chart in human terms the breadth and depth of the field. I have portrayed a spectrum of human situations drawn from experience that I believe are faithful to that which awaits a trainee or anyone else who would grapple seriously with the subject matter of the profession. All our theories, whether biological, psychological, or social, are in some sense meta-constructs that separate us from the realities of the lives we encounter. This is unavoidable, even necessary, for any helping profession. Yet to the degree that our theories and our routines and rituals separate us from the fundamental human data, we will have lost something.

For one thing, we will have lost a sense of the subtle privilege we enjoy as workers at the conjunction of nature and spirit. It is hazardous to refer to this privilege, and often enough one is simply waved away as a slushy sentimentalist when speaking of it. But I am not invoking sentiment here, rather I am simply declaring that those disorders that arise out of the toil of human development and that uniquely constrain its fulfillment are intrinsically challenging. For example, there is more that is biological than we would have ever supposed, yet even the biology has a distinctly human content and is always manifest in a human context. These are compelling intellectual issues, no doubt.

For another thing, we will have lost the capacity to assess realistically our technology and our progress. We are in the midst of scientific advances that hold out hope for ever greater therapeutic gains. Yet what member of our profession has not stopped to wonder if our therapeutics hold sufficiently in mind the person with the disorder? It has been sobering, for example, while rejoicing in the real progress in psychopharmacology, to confront the new realities spawned by deinstitutionalization and to take honest account of the formidable problems that may remain even after an individual no longer bears the symptomatic stigmata of major mental illness.

For yet another thing, we will have lost the potential for periodic renewal that is necessary for anyone who would make this field their life's work. A vocation in psychiatry requires such a capacity for periodic renewal. One cannot continuously confront lives in disarray without experiencing, to some degree, exhaustion, pessimism, and a waning enthusiasm. A capacity to step back and view afresh the human spirit at work in the lives of even our most desolate patients can become a balm for a weary professional.

It is important, therefore, that we not lose sight of the fundamental human data. From that data, a sample of which is collected here, lessons emerge. One lesson these accounts teach is of the kinship we all share in our fundamental needs, vulnerabilities, and strivings. Our field did not always accept this premise.

Originally we were known as alienists, because we looked after that *other* group of human beings whose outrageous behavior set them apart from the rest of us. It is now clear that behind the most bizarre mental phenomena is a human life afflicted, but with aspirations similar to our own. It is a fundamental task of the psychiatrist to find and engage this spirit and to keep it in view, whatever else he may do.

Secondly, the accounts remind us that such work is difficult. It is difficult because it addresses many forms of human unhappiness that must, in part, be borne in order to be understood and ameliorated. The bearing of unhappiness requires mentally that we sometimes walk with a slower gait and with stooped shoulders. (A teacher of mine once told me in a partly joking manner that I was not depressed enough to be a psychiatrist.) It is difficult also because expertise in this field requires personal life experience and reflection, not simply techique. Competence matures slowly, like wine. And it is finally difficult because we sometimes fail to help, despite our best efforts.

And lastly, the accounts bear witness to the importance of relationship, the power of human interaction to create, in varied settings and circumstances, emotions as apparently disparate as terror and love, loneliness and suffocation, hope and desolation. And it was, after all, the wonder of all this that first caught our eye and led us out in search of a sense of what truly matters in human lives.

INDEX